1/95   5⁰⁰

signed

The Chance to Say Goodbye

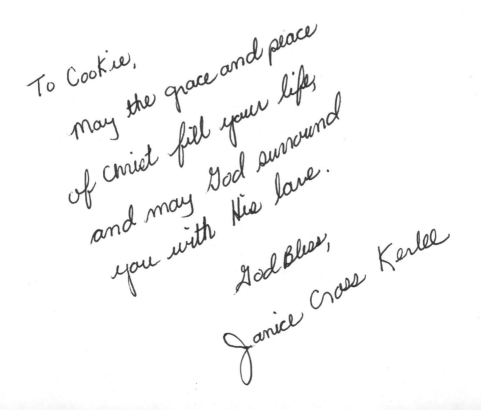

To Cookie,
May the grace and peace
of Christ fill your life,
and may God surround
you with His love.
        God Bless,
Janice Cross Kerlee

The Chance to Say Goodbye

Janice Cross Kerlee

Writers Club Press
San Jose New York Lincoln Shanghai

The Chance to Say Goodbye

Writers Club Press
an imprint of iUniverse.com, Inc.

For information address:
iUniverse.com, Inc.
5220 S 16th, Ste. 200
Lincoln, NE 68512
www.iuniverse.com

All events told in this story have been recorded as told to or remembered by the author. Slight variations from actual events are possible.

ISBN: 0-595-19034-0

Printed in the United States of America

Dedication

This book is dedicated to the memory of the Bonfire Twelve:

Miranda Denise Adams
Christopher David Breen
Michael Stephen Ebanks
Jeremy Richard Frampton
Jamie Lynn Hand
Christopher Lee Heard
Lucas John Kimmel
Bryan Allan McClain
Chad Anthony Powell
Jerry Don Self
Nathan Scott West
and
Timothy Doran Kerlee, Jr.

Epigraph

In the rising of the sun and in its going down,
  we remember them;
In the blowing of the wind and in the chill of winter,
  we remember them;
In the opening of the buds and in the warmth of summer,
  we remember them;
In the rustling of the leaves and the beauty of autumn,
  we remember them;
In the beginning of the year and when it ends,
  we remember them;
When we are weary and are in need of strength,
  we remember them;
When we have joys we yearn to share,
  we remember them;
So long as we live, they too shall live, for they are now a part of us,
  As we remember them.

"Gates of Prayer"
Reformed Judaism Prayer Book

Acknowledgements

I would first like to thank my dear friend, Susan Camp, who first suggested that I should write "Tim's Story" and started me on this eighteen-month project.

A word of thanks goes to Leisa Dear, Lyn Windsor, and Pat Sargeant, for correcting the grammar and sentence structure of my early work and encouraging me to "keep writing," and to Lawrence Smith for proofreading the finished product. I am also grateful for the patience of Pam Freni for answering my many questions about online publishing, and to Jay Sartain for his computer expertise.

My editor, Gerard Ferrell, took a raw tale and wove it into a moving story. To him I am extremely grateful.

Without the support of my loving husband, Tim, this book would not have been possible. Thank you, dear, for reading, encouraging and ungrudgingly giving up our time together.

Chapter 1

The Chance to Say Goodbye

"It is the quality of life that one leads
that gives it meaning and value; not its length."
Martin Luther King, Jr.

It was a typical July day in Memphis—hot and humid, the air thick enough to cut with a knife. Padding barefoot across the living room, I was thankful for the air conditioning. Even with it and every ceiling fan running, I still worked up a sweat doing housework. The heat was a blazing contrast from the previous week's crisp, cool air of Rocky Mountain National Park.

It had been a wonderful vacation. We'd driven to Las Vegas to drop our son, Tim, Jr., off for a week-long rafting excursion through the Grand

1

Canyon—his high school graduation present. While Tim rafted, my husband, Tim Sr., and I went on to California to visit his uncles. After picking up Tim, the three of us visited other relatives in Las Vegas before continuing our adventure—two weeks touring the beautiful Zion National Park, Bryce Canyon, Arches National Park and Rocky Mountain National Park. At Zion, Tim Jr. and I made the treacherous climb to Angel's Landing. We rode on horseback through Bryce Canyon, an exhilarating experience and one well worth the two days of soreness that followed. Then on to Rocky Mountain National Park, where we encountered a brief snowstorm and an up close meeting with a big-horned sheep. For my husband and I, Rocky Mountain National Park marked the end of our summer's traveling and a small sadness crept over us as it drew to a close. For Tim, Jr., one final trip remained before he would leave for college: a backpacking trip through Glacier National Park.

What a different summer 1999 had been from the year before, when I had spent six weeks helping care for my eighty-four year old mother, who was dying with cancer. It was the toughest thing that I had ever done in my life, but an experience I wouldn't have traded for anything. It gave me one last opportunity to spend quality time with Mom before the effect of her powerful painkillers made meaningful conversations at first difficult, then finally, impossible. We reminisced about the summer picnics, watermelon feasts, and backyard talent shows that my Pied Piper mother held for the neighborhood children. We discussed the antics, joys and problems of all of her grandchildren, and we rehashed the trip that she and my father had made to the Philippines to visit us when my husband and I lived there eighteen years before. One morning she said, "Although I wish the circumstances were different, I sure have enjoyed our time together." Mom was a wonderful Christian woman, and knowing that she was heaven-bound and released from her pain made her eventual death easier to bear. Naturally, I shed many tears. She was, after all, my mother. Yet, I was thankful to God for those final weeks together—thankful for the chance to say goodbye.

Going about my household chores that hot, humid Memphis day in 1999, I stopped suddenly in my tracks and thought, "Our life is perfect right now. I have a fantastic marriage and a wonderful son." After spending thirty-five years working for the Federal Government, my husband had retired four years earlier from his Civil Service job as a Personnel Manager, making long family vacations a reality. We had plenty of time for each other, and our marriage of twenty-one years was stronger than ever. Our son, Timothy Doran Kerlee, Jr., was a child any parent would be proud of. A top-notch student, especially gifted in mathematics, he graduated third in his class of more than six hundred thirty and scored 1510 out of 1600 on the Scholastic Aptitude Test (SAT). Fresh out of high school, he'd already earned 45 hours of college credit, through advanced placement classes and exams.

Along with excelling scholastically, Tim competed on academic teams, ran on the cross country team, held club offices, loved to swing dance and play ultimate Frisbee, was an Eagle Scout and recipient of the Explorer Scouts' highest honor, the Gold Award. He was very active in our church and admired by many for his talented portrayals as part of the youth acting group, ACTS (Actors for Christ through Theatre and Song.)

Tim's only difficulty in choosing a college was deciding upon one of the number of first class universities to which he'd been accepted. Yet, for this gifted, high achieving and well-rounded young man, the choice was easy: Texas A&M University, in College Station, Texas. The school's traditions and spirit, its emphasis on values and leadership, all appealed to Tim. He'd already decided to join its Corps of Cadets, an ROTC style student organization that stands at the heart of "Aggie tradition." A Commandant's Leadership Award, with its scholarship and the right to the lower Texas resident tuition, further added to the appeal of Texas A&M. He'd fallen in love with the school on his first campus visit, and the idea of graduating debt free sealed the deal. After visiting more than twenty-one colleges in search of his niche, Tim found it at Texas A&M. He would be an Aggie.

The air conditioner hummed and ceiling fans whirred overhead as I pondered this and our many other blessings. "Yes," I thought, "life is perfect— too perfect." The pain of my mother's death less than a year earlier still lingered, tempering my natural optimism. I wondered when the proverbial "other shoe" would drop. Standing in my Memphis living room, I little imagined how soon it would—or what a heavy one it would be.

The rest of the summer flew by and then Tim was leaving for college, to attend Texas A&M's annual "Fish Camp." "Fish" is Aggie talk for "freshman." I'm not sure where that term came from. Perhaps it is because a freshman is like a fish out of water; or maybe it's because "fish" sounds something like "frosh", an old fashion term for freshman. Fish Camp is a four-day orientation program for entering freshman, where they learn Texas A&M's history and traditions, and bond with each other in a variety of fun, challenging spirit building activities. It is said that the friendships made at Fish Camp last a lifetime. The experience helps perpetuate the strong loyalty to Texas A&M and to each other that has long been a hallmark of the university and the Aggie family. Well, Tim had a blast at Fish Camp and had two days to rest before starting Freshman Orientation Week.

Attendance at Fish Camp is optional for incoming freshmen. Freshmen Orientation Week—FOW—is mandatory for new cadets. Only about five percent of Texas A&M students belong to the Corps of Cadets, which harkens back to Texas A&M's days as an all-male military institution, yet the corps remains at the center of many of the school's traditions. Students who belong to the military style student organization are not required to enter the military after graduation, but FOW serves as a sort of "boot camp" for new cadets—who refer to it as "Hell Week." With Fish Camp and FOW both held before the start of the fall semester, Tim left for Texas in mid August.

His early departure posed a dilemma for me. The high school where I taught also began classes in mid August, forcing me to choose between missing the first few days of school to take Tim to Texas or letting him and my husband make the trip without me. My maternal instinct told me to take the trip: I'd spent seventeen years preparing Tim to leave the nest and fly on his own, and therefore felt I should be there right up to the moment he spread his wings. On the other hand, I know how critical it is for a teacher to be in his or her classes during the first few days of the school year. That's when the tone is set for the rest of the year, discipline established, and rules laid down. Missing even a few days in August could leave me unable to control my classes for the remainder of the year. Tim, ever the clear thinker, made my decision for me. Fearful of an emotional parting in Texas, he encouraged me to stay behind. It broke my heart, but I had to agree and let the two of them go off without me.

It wasn't long before "empty nest" syndrome set in. I'd always known it would be hard, but never imagined just how hard it would be. The demands on Tim's time during his first few weeks left him little time to call or e-mail, which only deepened the loneliness I felt for him. I cherished every call all the more because of the time between them. Although Tim loved Texas A&M and his professors, he seemed to hate the Corps during the first few weeks. During one Thursday night call, he sounded more nervous and upset than I'd ever heard him, and I feared he was on the verge of a breakdown. Panicky, I got very little sleep that night. Fortunately, he called again the next day and sounded much better. Maybe it's just that everything seems better on Fridays. I do know that during that stressful first month, he seriously considered leaving the Corps. We discussed the possibility of transferring to the University of Tennessee in the spring semester, and I remember telling him that we'd prayed for God to open doors to places where he belonged, and to keep closed those to where he didn't. "Everything has indicated that you should be at A&M and be in the Corps," I said. "I really think that you are where God wants you to be."

He agreed, saying simply, "I do too, Mom."

Eventually, Tim's natural determination and competitive spirit overcame his trepidation about the Corps. "I am going to lick the Corps," he said during one call. "It isn't going to lick me!"

In another: "Mom, I've decided that it's all a game."

"Son, we've told you that all along," I said.

"Yeah, but now I know the rules, and once I know the rules I'm as good as anybody playing a game." The rules called for sophomores in the Corps to train the fish. Once Tim had mastered the rules of "the game," he started enjoying it—seeking every opportunity to turn the tables on his superiors. It may have taken him a bit longer than others, but Tim finally seemed to be fitting in and looked forward to life as an Aggie.

Working on the annual Aggie Bonfire is widely considered one of the defining experiences of being an Aggie, and Tim was eager to be a part. Each fall, Texas A&M students build a towering log stack and burn it before the Thanksgiving weekend football game against the rival University of Texas Longhorns. Bonfire's flames represent the Aggies' "burning desire to beat the hell out of t.u."—the Aggies dismissive name for in-state rival UT. Aggies believe the Austin school is just "a" Texas university while Texas A&M is "the" university of Texas. Like most cadets, Tim had worked cutting down trees for the bonfire stack, and now couldn't wait to start construction.

In spite of his new positive outlook, he was looking forward to the campus visit we had planned at the end of October to attend a jazz concert and a football game. He told me something one night that I never thought I would hear.

"I miss you, Mom."

"I miss you, too, son."

"Don't take this wrong way," he added, "but if it weren't for the Corps, I wouldn't miss you nearly as much."

It rained all through the game, but we nonetheless had a great time on our weekend visit. The trip gave us our first look at the logs to be used for Bonfire. They were trees—big trees! The center pole, two telephone poles joined together to make a single post some sixty or more feet long around which the other logs would be stacked, was delivered that weekend, and Tim insisted on attending one of the traditional activities associated with that first step of construction. While he helped the Corps in a tug of war against the "non-regs" (students not in the Corps), we returned to our hotel to change clothes. After receiving some minor injuries in the frivolity, Tim decided against fully participating in the free-for-all activities. He later joked that he feared we'd kill him if we had to spend the weekend in an emergency room while he was treated for a broken bone. Instead, we took him and his girlfriend, Beth, out for dinner and a movie. A comment by Tim during dinner reflected both his renewed spirit and the last remnant of his homesickness: "It's only three weeks until you'll be here for Thanksgiving. Then it will be only three weeks until I'm home on Christmas break. I can do this!"

When we left, I gave him a big hug. I probably held on too long because he looked about ready to cry. Of course, he didn't. His friends were in his room, and he would never let them see him break down, not even for a second. But we left feeling that he looked good and that everything would be okay.

Tim's dream came true and he was working on the bonfire stack. He told me that he was going at night to work on it because there were fewer people then, and therefore he got better jobs that way. "Please, Tim," I begged, "Don't work on it at night. You need your sleep. When you don't get your sleep you get sick."

"I'm all right, Mom. When I work at night, I get to take a bag-in," he said, referring to the Corps practice of allowing cadets who work on bonfire at night to sleep in and therefore skip physical training and breakfast.

Another call brought news that he'd been promoted to "swing seat," a job that involved sitting on a dangling seat hung from the top of the stack and guiding each log as it was delivered up by crane to workers on the stack, who would then wire them into place. Sensing his excitement, I restrained my maternal instinct and masked my internal terror. Instead, I calmly said, "That sounds like fun, Tim."

"Oh, it is, Mom!" he answered. "It's lots of fun!"

Everything was going well. Tim had a straight-A average at midterm and had been voted October's Fish of Month for his unit. He was attending church regularly and had been cast in the lead of a play for Campus Crusade for Christ. And he had Beth—a steady girlfriend who was as sweet as she was beautiful. Yes, life was perfect, just as I'd believed that hot summer day in Memphis. And then the other shoe dropped.

It was the early morning of November 18th when I woke suddenly from a deep sleep. I glanced at the clock. It read 2:36 AM. An inner voice said, "Pray for Tim." I knew he was working nights on bonfire but had no idea what his schedule was. Remembering his description of "swing seat" and fearful of the danger it seemed to pose, I prayed. "Jesus, wrap your loving arms around Tim; send your angels to protect him, especially as he works on bonfire. Thank you for hearing my prayer. Amen." I started to go back to sleep, but suddenly I thought, "Maybe I was supposed to pray for Tim, my husband. He's going to Nashville for a state PTA board meeting." I said a quick prayer for his safety on his trip, and I went back to sleep. Less than two hours later, the phone rang. Tim had been hurt while working on the bonfire. He had a broken arm and maybe some other injuries, but was conscious as they transported him to the hospital. "Oh, no!" I thought. "I just knew Tim would manage to get hurt!"

Well, I knew I could handle a broken arm, but I remember thinking that the injury would put a crimp in our immediate plans. We'd already scheduled our trip to Texas for next week for Bonfire, Thanksgiving and the football game on Friday—but Tim Sr. also had a state PTA board meeting in Nashville that very day. I called for a substitute teacher, and we started getting ready for the ten-hour drive from our home in Bartlett, Tennessee to College Station. We still had no idea of the extent of what had happened just hours before, in the still early darkness of November 18, 1999. When I emerged from the shower, Tim, Sr. was sitting on the bed, sobbing and shaking. I sat beside him and tried to comfort him: "It's all right honey. It's just a broken arm." Suddenly, my heart jumped to my throat and my voice managed barely a croak. "Did you get another call while I was in the shower?" He just nodded. Frightened, I asked what he'd been told.

He replied with blurted-out fragments. "Doctor called…compound fracture of arm…broken hip…internal injuries…he's in shock…critical condition…getting ready to go into operating room…doctor said to stay by the phone." We clung to each other and cried for several minutes before he regained his composure and continued. "The doctor says it looks like a war zone in the hospital." Only now did I begin to grasp the enormity of the situation. I asked if others had been injured along with Tim, Jr. He nodded. Solemnly, his voice barely a whisper, he added, "The bonfire collapsed."

Instantly I remembered the sight of those enormous logs waiting to be stacked, six tiers high to resemble a huge wooden wedding cake. What had Tim Jr. told us? Fifty-five or sixty feet tall when complete? The thought of it collapsing caused me to shudder.

We began making phone calls. Among the first was one to our pastor, Rick Kirchoff, who immediately came to our home and prayed and waited with us for two and a half hours that seemed endless. We turned on the television, to learn that several students had already been pronounced dead. I fell to my knees and wailed in grief for the parents of those students. At least Tim, Jr. was alive. My belief that God had a special plan for him came to mind, and was reinforced. I thought back to our running household joke, an exchange between Tim and me. "Now when you get to the White House…" I would begin. Tim would shoot back, "Mom, I'm too **honest** to be a politician." Once, I turned the exchange serious. "This country needs a strong, intelligent Christian as President," I said. This seemed to sadden him, although he agreed. "But you have to get elected first," he replied. Maybe he wouldn't be president, but I remained convinced that God had some wonderful plan for him. Surely, the Lord would pull our son through this tragedy so that Tim could accomplish major tasks for his kingdom.

The call from the doctor finally came. Tim was stable, but his condition was very tenuous. He'd suffered a crushed pelvis and extensive internal injuries. The doctor offered no guarantees; he only urged us to come as quickly as we could.

As Rick, our pastor from Germantown United Methodist Church, drove us to the airport, my husband said, "I don't know what to do." I found my answer in scripture. Quoting 1 Thessalonians 5:17, I encouraged him to "Pray without ceasing." I don't believe I'd ever really understood that passage before. But from the moment of the doctor's call, my every thought had become a plea to God.

Since leaving home, Tim, Jr. had become an affiliate member of A&M United Methodist Church. They'd already been contacted by our home church and apprised of the situation. We arrived at Tim's hospital bedside about one in the afternoon to find him conscious and being ministered to by Laurinda Kwiatkowski, A&M United Methodist's youth director and Tim's Sunday School teacher. I little knew it then, but this blonde- headed cherub and mother of four would prove to be one of God's angels on earth. Other than Thursday evening at home with her family, she would remain by our sides for the remainder of the ordeal at the hospital. Without her compassionate, loving and guiding spirit, I'm not sure we could have made it.

By the time we arrived, Timothy had already received over 100 units of blood and blood products. The doctor told us that he had almost lost Tim three times on the operating table. Timothy tried to speak, despite the breathing tube in his throat. He responded to us with nods, raised eyebrows, blinks, or squeezes of our hands. His condition seemed better than we'd dared to hope. Twice, tears welled in his eyes and we asked if he was in pain. Nodding an affirmative, he was given pain medication. Later, an IV drip would administer a steady dose of pain-relieving morphine.

Conversations with the doctor offered little hope. So we refused to listen. Instead, we drew our hope from knowing that hundreds of people were praying to God (who, after all, had some special plan for Tim and for whom all things are possible).

The doctors had tried to stop Tim's internal bleeding, but once the body starts bleeding so profusely, stopping it is difficult. They had repaired some major organs, but his pelvis was completely crushed. All they could do was wrap and bind his abdomen. His left leg also posed a major problem: several inches were missing from a severed vein, and all the doctors could do was tie it off. Dealing with these major injuries was foremost in the doctors' minds. The compound fracture of his right arm was considered minor by comparison; it could be set later. Once Tim showed signs of improvement, we were assured by Dr. Steve Cox, treatment would be as aggressive as safely possible.

"First we get him well, then we talk reconstructive surgery for that hip, right?" I optimistically replied to this assurance. The doctor looked taken aback, then just nodded.

That afternoon, we allowed a few of Tim's friends to visit him. The rest kept vigil in the ICU waiting room, the halls and the hospital basement, where food and cots were provided for family and friends of the injured. Tim, Sr. and I took turns going to the waiting room to collect phone messages, take calls and comfort the waiting students, who seemed to flock to us like chicks to a mother hen. Laurinda noted that our visits with the students seemed to revitalize and energize Tim, Sr. and I whenever we appeared exhausted. We all formed a close bond that day.

Tim's "old lady" (Corps talk for "roommate"), Triwahyu ("Tree") Widodo, an international student from Indonesia, was having a particularly difficult time dealing with survivor's guilt. It seems Tim had traded places about ten minutes before the collapse with a buddy named Derek Woodley. Tim had convinced Woodley that the "swing seat" was a ton of fun and that he should try it. Tree had helped Tim get up to the fourth stack and then returned to the ground. He was standing beside another student when the stack fell. Tree ran one way; the other student ran another way. Tree thought that the other student had been killed instantly by falling logs, and he had escaped unharmed. "I was very bad, mum," he later told me. "I ran."

"It's good you ran, Widodo," I replied. "You did the right thing. There was nothing else you could do."

"But I left my buddy, mum. I should never have left my buddy. I did bad."

I explained that had he stayed with his buddy, his parents would have been among those already grieving their lost children, and he should be thankful that he had run the right way.

"Tim has a lot or respect for you, Widodo," I continued. "It takes courage to come to another country, learn the language, and profess a completely different faith (Buddhism) from most of those around you."

"I know Tim Kerlee likes me, mum. He gives me lots of hugs."

The students, who took turns answering the phone, marveled at the number of calls we received. At one point, Tim, Sr. walked into the waiting room to overhear the following exchange between two of our son's buddies:

"Who was that?"

"That was his barber. Can you believe it? I don't even know my barber's name!"

Twice during those long two days, I took calls from Clay Bailey, a reporter for the Memphis *Commercial Appeal*, our local newspaper. Both my husband and I have a great deal of respect for Clay, and so I agreed to the telephone interviews. Clay hated to intrude, but said the paper's phone lines were jammed with calls asking about Tim. He had to know more about a 17-year-old who could have this much impact on a community. I knew the folks at home would want to know the latest news about Tim and this seemed a good way to keep them informed. I was happy to talk about Tim, but withheld comments about the university or the accident itself.

Sometimes it was necessary for both my husband and me to leave Tim's room. During one of these intervals we talked to another Aggie parent,

William Hutchinson, who had a child in ICU because of the bonfire accident. His son, Chad, was severely bruised and had hit his head. Chad had been X-rayed and was under observation for a possible concussion. He had fallen about forty feet, but doctors had found none of the internal injuries they believed he would have suffered. They also feared he was delusional because he insisted his mother had caught him. Hearing his son's explanation, William immediately understood. His wife had died four years ago, and Chad had always wondered why his mother had to die. "Now I know," he told his father. "She died so she could catch me today."

Most of Tim's squadron from the Corps of Cadets stayed through the night. Many never left during his forty-eight hours in the hospital. Their loyalty was amazing. They certainly lived the school's motto, "Through Unity, Strength." Laurinda had them write messages and delivered their notes to Tim. Her ministry was becoming twofold, as would ours. Our first ministry was to Tim, the second to his buddies. Our ministry to ourselves would have to wait.

It was a long night. At one point, my heart beat so hard and fast I thought it would pound right out of my chest. A nurse checked my blood pressure: a little high, but reasonable under the circumstances. Tim, Sr. and I alternated catnaps. Once during the night, I left the room to sit in a chair by the desk in the ICU ward. I had tried to be strong for my son, my husband and the students, but exhaustion and anxiety finally overwhelmed me. I loosed my emotion and cried almost hysterically. It was then that I hit rock bottom. My cup emptied, the Lord could now replenish it.

There's a recent version of the New Testament called *The Message*. It doesn't claim to be a translation. Instead, it is the Bible in contemporary language. Its paraphrase of the first Beatitude reads, "You're blessed when you are at the end of your rope. With less of you, there is more of God and his rule." These words help me understand why "a good cry" is often helpful. If we give our burdens to Christ, knowing we are helpless, then we can carry on with His strength. I had truly reached the end of my rope. I was, I realized then, truly blessed because God could take control of my life.

I returned to Tim's room, knelt by his bedside, and surrendered my son to God. There was nothing more the doctors could do. His life was in the Lord's hands. Although I wanted desperately for Tim to live on earth, I told God that I would accept His decision for Tim's future.

The next morning brought us hope. Tim had made it through the night. In itself, this had been a major accomplishment. It also appeared that the amount of blood in his urine had decreased and his heartbeat, though high, was steady. His pulse was normal. We thought things were looking up. Then Dr. Cox came and took us aside. He was such a compassionate, loving doctor. His genuine concern for Tim as a person, not simply a patient, showed in the difficulty he had looking us in the face as he broke the news. Funny the things you notice at a time like that, but I remember him fingering a paper clip as he spoke, watching the shiny tiny wire in his hand and only glancing at us occasionally.

He was clearly heartbroken to tell us the truth about Tim's condition. The tied-off vein in his leg was causing a problem. Blood could reach the foot, but not return to the heart. This caused it to pool in his leg. Toxins were developing in our son's young body and his kidneys were failing. Other organs most likely would follow. Amputation appeared the only solution, but further surgery was impossible in Tim's weakened condition. That option removed, our only remaining decision was whether to continue giving him blood products in hope of adding a few hours to his life. Typically in a critical case, patients receive forty to fifty units of blood and blood products before hope is abandoned. Tim, Jr. already had received 183 units.

The harsh reality of the preceding day crossed into the surreal. This couldn't be happening to our son! Would someone please wake us up from this nightmare? Once more, Tim, Sr. and I clung to each other in overwhelming tears. Our son had been at the center of our world for nearly eighteen years, and now that world was crumbling around us. Faced with the hardest decision of our lives, Tim, Sr. shared his confidence that our son would go to heaven. "I don't want him to go through hell to get there," he said. Assured that our son would suffer no pain, we declined the amputation and halted administering blood products. Tim, Jr. would pass into a coma and thence peacefully into God's hands.

The doctor told nurses to allow anyone we wanted in to see Tim. I realized then that he had known from the beginning that our son would not survive. All of his hard work had served to give us the chance to say good-bye.

After telephoning relatives, I went out into the waiting room. I gathered Tim's friends around me, then broke the news that he was dying. Having nursed my mother through the final weeks of her life, I had read the books from Hospice and knew— intellectually—what I should do. Emotionally, however, I was far from prepared for this moment. As we began the most difficult task imaginable for parents, preparing our child for death, we relied heavily upon the gentle guidance of Tim's youth pastor, Laurinda. Not only was Laurinda a youth minister, but she was also a trained hospital chaplain. She compassionately walked us through the steps of the death process.

Our son's life had been a beautiful and spiritual experience. We felt deeply that his death should be no different. Friends had always been so important to him, and so he and they should have one last chance to see each other. Brent Clayton, Timothy's best friend at A&M, and Timothy's girlfriend, Beth Priolo, were among the first group in to see him. Also with them was Melynda Knowles, Brent's girlfriend and Beth's roommate. Collectively, I had dubbed them "the fantastic four" because of the closeness of their friendship. Together again, near this all too sudden end, Brent took Timothy's hand. Refusing to accept the reality, he urged our son to squeeze his hand and to fight. Tim shook his head, no. Laurinda spoke. "Are you tired, Tim?" she asked. Tim raised his eyebrows. His eyes popped open and he nodded emphatically. Laurinda took me aside. "People can usually sense when they are dying," she said gently. "He needs to be told."

His friends left the room. I turned to Tim and softly rubbed his head. I told him, "You don't have to fight anymore, Tim. It's okay. You really tried, but this accident was too big, your injuries too great. You don't have to fight. You can go home to Jesus." Tears came from his eyes. He shook his head "no" when Laurinda asked if he was in pain. Timothy was crying because he did not want to die. His love of life was genuine. He experienced the joy of living with a fullness that few can imagine. Again Laurinda spoke, this time addressing me. "He needs reassurance of where he's going, and it's okay for you to cry and to let him know you are going to miss him." I wiped his tears and spoke to him gently. "I know, Buddy. We're going to miss you, too. We love you so much, and we are going to miss you so much. But if you think Aggieland is wonderful, and the Aggie spirit is great, you just wait until you get to heaven and get to be with Jesus. It's going to be so wonderful."

We cried together and told him that it would be hard for us, but that we would make it. I knew that, among other things, he was worried about us—his father and me. The three of us had always been so close. We'd shared so many wonderful experiences together. Memories of the previous summer's trip returned. A few months now seemed ages ago. It had been the second of our family's western excursions, during which we'd visited almost all of the major National Parks that side of the Mississippi. We had lived a year in Italy, traveling that country, and had also visited England, France, Germany, and Austria.

Our relationship as parents and child had been a remarkably peaceful one. Tim, Sr., and I could count on one hand the number of arguments typical between teenagers and their parents. Nor was he, unlike so many of his contemporaries, shy or reluctant to show his affection for us. For example, my husband's retirement job of substitute teaching would often result in an assignment in our son's school. Rather than avoiding his father as most teenagers would do, Tim, Jr., would go out of his way to stop by and visit for a few minutes. My husband often attended scouting functions and campouts, on which he and Tim occasionally bunked together.

The two of us would walk the street, arm-in-arm, or him with an arm draped over my shoulder. Without his support and encouragement, I doubt I'd have made the previous summer's climb to the top of Angel's Landing at Zion National Park. While cooking supper at home, I frequently would be interrupted with an impromptu swing dance session in the kitchen. Not the actions of your average teenage boy!

What, then, could it have been like for this seventeen-year-old, with such zest for life and everything to live for, to be told he was dying? Yet, those were his only tears. A sense of peace and calm seemed to wash over him. I wish we could have talked. I thought of asking to remove his breathing tube so we could communicate, but the struggle for him to breathe would have been too hard on him at the last. Knowing we could no longer have him with us, we were determined for his end to be peaceful. Even unable to speak, Tim managed to get his point across. Individually or in small groups, his friends came in to say goodbye. His Fish Camp counselors came in to talk about the positive influence he had been during their camp, with his school spirit and enthusiasm. The Campus Crusade for Christ's theater director said she had cast him as the lead in the play "David" because, like David, he really was a "man after God's own heart."

Other fish in his squadron shared how much they admired and looked up to him. He was their leader. Upperclassmen spoke of what an outstanding "fish" he was, telling how senior cadets would practice the Corps' obstacle course at night—determined not to be beaten again by "fish Kerlee." They also told him that he'd earned his Corps Brass, and that it was being engraved right at the moment. Representing hard work and the respect of upperclassmen cadets, Corps Brass is the first corps award that a fish cadet can receive. "You earned it a long time ago," they told him. "We were just waiting for some of your buddies to catch up with you."

Tim's hand started shaking. It seemed to me that he was asking for his brass, and I asked him if that is what he wanted. He replied with an emphatic nod. In a manner befitting the Corps Commander himself, I immediately dispatched the cadets to go get Tim's brass. "Go to the front of the line when you get back," I ordered. They hightailed it out of there and were back in about thirty minutes with Tim's Corps Brass. We held it out for him and he tried to open his eyes and focus, but his eyesight was fading. Placing it in his hand, I wrapped his weak fingers around the shiny metal for him to feel it. Aware of the Corps' strict dress code, I reassured him, "Don't worry about the fingerprints. I'll polish the brass later."

In between visitors, Tim, Sr. and I managed to get some private moments with our son. To this day, I can hear my husband repeatedly saying, "I love you, boy." Never before had the word "boy" resonated with such affection and tenderness. Tenderly and with affection, I gently rubbed his hand. Tim had always loved to have his head rubbed, especially when his hair was cut short—and a fish haircut is nothing if not short. Suddenly, his hand moved away as if annoyed. At first I was bewildered, then it dawned on me. "Tim," I asked, "are you trying to tell me that you want your head rubbed, not your hand?" Another affirmative nod, this one noticeably weaker. Tim, Sr. and I then took turns gently rubbing his head. Quietly, we recounted stories of family vacations and other special times we'd shared: trips to Boy Scout National Jamborees, to the National Scout Reservation at Philmont and his graduation trip rafting through the Grand Canyon. We'd kissed him frequently since the beginning of the ordeal, despite the difficulty of maneuvering around the many tubes, wires, and other medical equipment. I feared startling him with a kiss and causing him to jerk something out of place, so we warned him of each imminent kiss with, "incoming!" Laurinda has since told us that she came to love the expression and now uses it with her children.

Sitting in Tim's hospital room hearing his friends' many accolades, I thought of his humble spirit. He would never have told these stories about himself, and hearing them now was probably embarrassing to him. Some of the comments provoked startled looks on his face. Tim's lifelong reluctance to "toot his own horn" was ordinarily a good trait, but proved a hindrance when filling out scholarship applications. Once, while discussing how well-liked he was by teachers, scout leaders, church youth workers, and other adults with whom he had contact, Tim shared his inner bewilderment. "I don't understand why everybody thinks I'm special. There's nothing special about me. I just do what everybody should do."

"*Should* is the operative word, son," I replied. "Most of us know what we should do, but we don't always do it."

In the hospital, I reminded him of the universal high regard with which he was held. "You see, sweetie, I told you that you were special. You've just been an angel in disguise." When I made a similar comment to Laurinda, she corrected me. "Janice, you've got that wrong." Initially puzzled, I smiled when I realized her meaning. "There's no disguise," we said in unison.

Unable to speak, Tim's brain must have been working overtime to try to find ways to communicate. I was holding his hand and it started jerking like he was trying to squeeze mine, when he mouthed the word, "Mom." Even without words, I knew his meaning. As a small child, I had taught him a silent code that I had learned as a young girl from my own mother. When speaking aloud was inappropriate, such as in church, three squeezes of the other's hand would signal, "I love you"—one squeeze for each word. With speech now impossible, I asked if he was trying to signal that he loved me. Tim nodded. "I love you, too," I said, giving him my husband's hand. "And here is Dad's hand so you can tell him."

Later that afternoon, just hours after receiving his Corps Brass as a deserving fish, Tim was further honored by members of his squadron with the presentation of his senior boots and saber. For those unfamiliar with Texas A&M and its tradition-bound corps, the significance of a pair of boots may be difficult to comprehend. For three years, the standard cadet uniform includes straight-legged trousers and black Oxfords. Seniors, however, wear jodhpurs and highly polished, custom-made brown riding boots. The presentation of senior boots to a fish, therefore, reflects the ultimate regard in which the senior cadets held our son. His sight by now gone, we put his hands upon the boots and saber for him to feel them. In recognition of his 4.0 GPA at midterm, they also presented him with the

Scholastic Cord, which is awarded to the unit with the highest GPA, and a medal for having at least a 3.5 average.

Tim was extremely tired and weak after his long ordeal. When I asked if he wanted us to bring in more of his friends, his nod was hesitant. We began admitting groups of eight to ten at a time, in an effort to allow as many people to say their farewells in less time and give Tim more time to rest. By now, Tim's professors were among the visitors and even they wanted to tell Tim how much he meant to them and how much they admired him. No eulogy could have been a more beautiful celebration of his spirit. Again and again, we heard of his constant efforts to cheer up his friends when they were down. He would do anything, even make himself look silly, to get someone to smile. He knew the power of a smile.

When Tim was too tired to see visitors, we read the cards that elementary students had written and described the pictures to him. One in particular was especially meaningful: a drawing of a large heart with the Texas A&M logo in the middle and an eagle's head coming from the top and its wings from the side. The feathers of the eagle intersected the heart, forming small crosses. That picture seemed to capture the very spirit of Tim. His big heart was full of love for people—all people—and he only wanted the best for everyone. He had fun in everything he did and always tried to include others in his activities, and encouraged them to make the most of the experience. The eagle had been his personal symbol ever since becoming an Eagle Scout; he loved Texas A&M since first setting foot on its campus, and Christ was in every aspect of his life. We sensed the guiding hand of the Holy Spirit in that drawing by the elementary school student, a young boy named Roosevelt Walker.

In little more than a day since leaving Memphis after the accident, we had become so close with so many people whom we'd never before met that it was impossible to feel alone throughout our ordeal. Less than 100 miles from College Station, in Waco, was another Memphis resident who shared in our personal grief. A high-school friend of his, Jessica Wicke, was now attending Baylor University and when word of the collapse reached home, hundreds of their former schoolmates began contacting her for news of his condition. They figured that since she was in Texas, she might have a better idea of what was going on. Jessica made the drive to College Station, arriving at the hospital a few hours before Tim died. In the previous twenty-four hours, she told him, she'd gotten more e-mail messages than in the previous year. "You would not believe all the people who told me to send you their love and let you know they've been praying for you," she said.

Tim clung to life for twelve hours after we halted the blood products. He'd always had a very hardy constitution and the months of Corps training had him in the best physical shape he'd ever been. His strong young body was refusing to release its grip on the life he loved so dearly. I reminded him of the reward that awaited him for how he'd expressed that love. "When you get to Heaven and are standing in the presence of God, you are going to wonder why you fought so hard to stay here on earth." A slight smile crossed his face. We prayed and sang hymns.

"Something about That Name," gave me particular comfort:

> Jesus, Jesus, O-oh Jesus, oh there's something about that name.
> Master, Savior, Jesus; it's like the fragrance after the rain.
> Jesus, Jesus, O-oh Jesus, let all heaven and earth proclaim.
> Kings and kingdoms will all pass away,
> But there's something about that name.

Jesus' name never seemed so sweet. We recited the 23rd Psalm and quoted other scripture. Romans 8:38-39 was frequently repeated: "For I am convinced that neither death nor life, neither angels nor demons, neither the present nor the future, nor any powers, neither height nor depth, not anything else in all creation, will be able to separate us from the love of God that is in Christ Jesus our Lord." We could not just sit back and wait for Tim to die. We did everything we could to make his death a spiritual and meaningful experience, and to reassure him not only of the love family and friends had for him, but also of God's love.

About six o'clock that evening, my husband brought Tim word that his half-brother from Virginia was coming to see him. "Sean's coming to see you, Buddy. He should be here in about two hours." Tim dearly loved Sean and had always looked up to him. He'd been looking forward to spending Christmas with Sean and his wife, Tracy, and their twins, Payton and Lincoln. Tim hadn't seen his niece and nephew since they were nine months old; they were now two and half years old. We didn't know at the time, but Tim's half-sister, Michele, was also coming. A few minutes later, a nurse came into the room to tell us our son had only about an hour to live. My heart sank. Had Tim heard and understood his Dad's news about Sean? I hoped not.

The presence of God in that room became overwhelming. I have had mountaintop experiences before; moments when I have felt the joy and power of the Holy Spirit in my life and extreme closeness to God, but none compared to this. We felt as if we were standing in the presence of the Almighty, and that He was there not only for Tim but also to assure us of Tim's future in His presence and among the angels. I'm convinced that Tim was seeing angels already—and everywhere around him.

I believe strongly in angels. My prayer at two that morning, with its call for angels to protect Tim, had not been just words. My belief in angels had been reaffirmed several years before by the testimony of a fellow church member, a hospital nurse. She had been called to the room of a dying young girl, to assist her in the bathroom. The girl's grandmother also was there, and when the child asked her grandmother if she was going to die, the woman answered, "Why would you ask that?"

"Because," the child said, "there are two angels sitting at the foot of my bed." That simple testimony forever swept from my mind, heart and soul any doubt I may have had.

Surrounded by angels and in the overwhelming presence of God, Tim began his departure from this world. Gradually, his pulse and heartbeat slowed to an eventual flatline. Then, suddenly, his body jumped and his heartbeat and pulse returned almost to normal. This happened twice more and I told him, "I know you're trying to hang on to see Sean. It's okay, Tim. Sean will understand. You can go on home." Minutes later, he breathed his last, and we kissed our son goodbye.

Chapter 2

Peace in the Midst of Grief

"And God will raise you up on eagle's wings,
Bear you on the breath of dawn,
Make you to shine like the sun,
And hold you in the palm of God's hand."
On Eagles' Wings

Tim died on November 19, 1999, at 8:00 p.m. After Tim, Sr. and I said our final goodbyes, we went out to the ICU waiting room and gathered his friends around us. Gently, I announced, "He's gone home, folks."

One of his buddies commented, "Tim is the Twelfth Man." Non-Aggies may take that to mean that Tim had been the last of the bonfire tragedy's dozen victims. But to students at Texas A&M, the phrase holds deeper meaning. Among the Aggies' many traditions, students stand up through football games to demonstrate their support for the team and symbolizing the ready willingness to take their place on the field.

The original "twelfth man" was a Texas A&M student named E. King Gill. Down to his last reserve player in a 1922 game against Centre College, the No. 1 team in the nation, Coach Dana X. Bible asked Gill if he would play if needed. Although not on the team, Gill suited up and stood on the sidelines for the second half. He never got into the game, which the Aggies won, 22-14, but inadvertently began what today is considered one of the nation's finest college football traditions.

In a larger sense, however, the tradition of the Twelfth Man represents Aggies' commitment to the university and to each other; and their ready willingness to help any Aggie in need. It is often used to refer to the entire student body—more than 40,000 strong. To refer to Tim individually as the Twelfth Man, therefore, was quite a compliment.

We embraced Tim's friends and held them while they cried. Later, a squadron mother wrote that Tim, Sr. and I seemed to "have a glow" around us. I'm not surprised. That glow was God's love, with which we were surrounded. When Moses came down from Mount Sinai, his face glowed so much from having seen God face-to-face that he wore a veil to avoid frightening his people. We had not seen God, but His presence was almost tangible. Months after Tim's death, another squadron mom who'd been at the hospital that night said it was "obvious that we had experienced something." What we'd experienced was God's presence in that hospital room; He had carried us for the previous two days and would do so for many days to come.

During those two days, Laurinda and I discussed what we would do after Tim passed away. His many companions could not simply be sent home after their two-day vigil of loyalty and love. Some sort of closure was needed, and we'd planned a short memorial service in the hospital chapel. We set it for nine o'clock that night, and silently prayed that Sean would arrive by then. Another round of phone calls to family, then we went out to face the reporters waiting in the hospital parking lot.

On our way outside, Laurinda said she'd seen the Holy Spirit give me the right words to say to Tim all day. "I'm sure He will give you the right words now," she added.

"Laurinda, who do you think Tim, Jr. got his love of acting from? I've performed many times in front of crowds. TV cameras don't scare me," I replied.

Besides, I had just stood in the presence of God. He hadn't let me down then and He won't let me down now, I thought. It was miraculous. In a sense, Tim, Sr. and I seemed more composed than the reporters who interviewed us did.

Several asked if they could attend the memorial service. We said they were welcome, but that cameras and notebooks were not. One response in particular will never leave me: "Oh, no. I just want to be a part of this."

By the time Tim, Sr. and I arrived in the chapel, it was filled beyond capacity; the heat was stifling. Laurinda suggested moving to the lobby and cadets immediately went to work collecting chairs and sofas to sit on. With some two hundred people present, space was tight. Many stood at the very edges of the lobby; some sat on the floor. The hospital chaplain opened with a few words, followed by Laurinda. Then we sang "Amazing Grace." At least I think we did; everything was such a blur.

Tim, Sr. then talked to the young people about their need to support each other and be there for each other throughout this trying time. It was during his brief comments that I received the inspiration for my talk. It went something like this:

> When Tim, Jr. was about eight years old, my husband accepted a job in Italy. We didn't know exactly how Tim would take the news. When we told him, his enthusiastic response was, 'Now I can go to Florence and see Michaelangelo's *David* in person.'
>
> And what role was Tim going to play for Campus Crusade's play? Yes, that's right, David. We've heard many times today that Tim was

so much like David because Tim, like David, was a man after God's own heart. But many times David was confused, and he had many doubts. Tim had many questions and doubts as well. But he never stopped seeking answers. It's okay to have doubts; it's human; it's natural. But be sure to surround yourself with people who can help you with those questions, who can work with you through your doubts. Now, more than ever, you will need that help.

Then I asked for "Tim stories." I wanted the students to leave with good memories and some positive feelings—to take with them some part of Tim that would remain forever. Echoing the words of the Campus Crusade for Christ theater director and affirming the theme of my brief talk, a fellow crusade member said that Tim "was like David. He was a man after God's own heart. He really loved the Lord with his whole being."

Many of the cadets present emphasized Tim's standing in the squadron, as leader of the fish. He was responsible. He was determined. "Whenever we had to get something done, we went to Tim" is one remark that stands out in my mind. Others praised Tim's intelligence, with one sophomore declaring him "smarter than some of the upperclassmen." Hearing this, Maj. Gen. "Ted" Hopgood, the retired U.S. Marine who serves as Commandant of the Corps of Cadets, rolled his eyes, smiled, stifled a laugh and mouthed, "Some?" When his turn to speak came, however, the general also focused on the serious. Tim had outstanding character, abilities and promise, he said. His death had been a great loss to the Corps.

One of Tim's Aggie mentors, Jim Wheeler, had flown from Memphis to be with us during this ordeal. Jim is an "Old Ag,"—a graduate who remains active with Texas A&M and alumni association activities. Jim lives in Germantown, and serves on the university's Corps Advisory Board. He had hand delivered Tim's Corps scholarship award, and he related his early encounters with our son with a touch of humor. "When I first read Tim's profile, I thought he was a nerd," he began. "I didn't think he would ever make it in the Corps. Then I met Tim. The next day, I called General Hopgood and told him that Tim was a future Corps Commander."

These testimonies were wonderful, but I had heard enough serious stories. I told the cadets that it was a shame they never got to know the wild and crazy side of Tim. I told how he had dressed up as Cher to lip-sync a song at a church banquet honoring the youth workers. In a well-padded (and tight!) dress and four-inch heels, he came down from the stage to work the crowd. When he sat in the lap of a male counselor, he brought down the house with laughter. I insisted on hearing some funny stories. That was all the prompting they needed. Anyone who knew Tim well had a humorous tale to tell.

Nenna, a lovely young lady (yes, the Corps is coed) in Tim's squadron, told this story in her beautiful Nigerian accent. It took place one Saturday when the squadron was planting trees to replace those used for the bonfire. "When we got away from the rest of the squadron, Tim was dancing while he dug holes and planted. He had some moves! I told him, 'You dance *goooood* for a white boy.'" Of course this created tremendous laughter, and that was just what we needed!

Kelly, the director of "David," told us how Tim helped her overcome a problem with the play—one resulting from women having been cast in male roles to compensate for a shortage of male actors. A scene involving a hug between David (Tim) and Samuel, played by a young woman, "just didn't look right. It wasn't a manly hug." Kelly asked Tim if he'd ever hugged a man, to which he said he hugged his father all the time. "Well, just pretend she's your Dad," she remembered telling him. Tim stepped back, looked the young lady over, and shook his head. "Naaaw," he said. "I don't *think* so."

Another big laugh, and we were on a roll. Fish Widodo was next. He told us about the time he and Tim had a commitment immediately prior to an inspection and had asked their buddies to help them out by putting the "finishing touches" on their clean uniforms. They arrived at the residence hall to find their uniforms hanging, brass and nametags securely in place and everything seemingly up to standard. Quickly changing into their fresh uniforms, they took their places in the inspection line. All would have gone well, except for the difference in height between Tim and Widodo—and their buddies having put Tim's nametag on Widodo's uniform and vice-versa. During the ensuing chewing out, Tim looked down to find he was wearing trousers about six inches short, while Widodo's bagged around his ankles. This story particularly amused the upperclassmen, who'd not witnessed the prank.

Even without the pranks played upon them by upperclassmen—especially the sophomores charged with their training—the life of a Corps fish can be trying. For one thing, they're all referred to as "fish," and never by their given names. Unlike upperclassmen, who are assigned rooms in Corps residence halls, their quarters are simply called "holes." The official meeting place for fish is known as "the fallout hole." Tim and Widodo lived in the fallout hole.

Along with learning a seemingly whole new language, a typical day for fish begins with early morning physical training and ends late at night with shoe shining and brass polishing after required study hours. What rest they get during non-study hours is frequently interrupted by the unexpected appearance in their holes by sophomores and upperclassmen—at which time the fish are required to jump to attention. Consequently, afternoon naps are hard to come by, and the reason why fish Chattaway's tale proved so amusing to so many of the cadets at the memorial.

"I walked into the fallout hole to ask Kerlee about something. I didn't see anyone, so I started to walk out. I thought I heard something and turned around. No one was there. I turned to leave again, and this time I thought I heard a faint 'Chattaway!' I turned back again and saw nothing. I thought it was my imagination and started to leave once more. All of a sudden, Kerlee popped out from under the rack (bunk), and says, 'What do you need, Chattaway?' " Tim's sudden appearance startled his fellow fish, who told him to *never* scare him like that again and asked why he was under the bunk.

"Sorry, Chattaway," he replied, "I was just trying to catch a nap."

After many delightful Tim stories, I closed with a Tim and Widodo story from our October visit—the weekend of the home game against Oklahoma State. After breakfast on the morning of the game, we brought Tim back to his "hole" to get ready for the pre-game inspection. Tim invited us for the inspection, and so we watched as the "fish of the day" stood in the hallway, blew a bugle and twenty-five fish piled into the corridor. It was raining, and the sophomores sent them back to their holes to put on their rain gear.

At the second call, everyone immediately hustled back into the corridor—except Tim and Widodo. When they finally appeared from their hole, they slammed themselves up against the wall for inspection. The sophomores conducting the inspection spared them a chewing out for their tardiness, perhaps because his father and I were there. The reason remained a mystery until late that night, when we brought Tim back to our hotel room. Overcome by curiosity, I finally asked what had caused the delay.

Tim began to laugh as he explained: Widodo had tried to put on his rain gear by slipping it over his head, rather than unfastening it and refastening it once it was on. His head got stuck in the ventilation flap on the inside of the coat, which Tim had to pull off of him and then help him slip back into. Tim said, "Next time, Widodo, just unfasten it."

Widodo snapped back with a resounding "No, me too lazy." As we laughed, Tim quipped, "You know, Mom. It's pretty funny at midnight, but it sure wasn't funny this morning."

That story just about wrapped up the service, and after thanking everyone for coming and sharing their memories of Tim, we ended by singing Tim's personal theme song, "On Eagle's Wings." I know Tim was looking down from heaven and smiling. It was just the way he would want to have been remembered. Knowing that and hoping that the previous hours had given the young people there some happy memories made Laurinda, Tim, Sr. and me smile.

Just after the service, Sean, Michele and her husband, Pete, bounded through the hospital's front door and grabbed us. I hugged Sean tight and asked, "Do you know?" He said he didn't know anything. I told him Tim had died and that we'd just finished a memorial service. I asked if he wanted to go upstairs to see Tim and all of us went up to his room. The nurses had removed all the tubes and machinery and cleaned him up for us. Sean was upset because he hadn't gotten there in time to see Tim alive. He said he was angry with God because he felt that God had told him Tim would still be alive when he got to the hospital. I wasn't upset with this; anger is a natural reaction to grief. I told Sean how Tim had tried to hang on to see him, but that I had told Tim to go on home to Jesus and that his brother would understand. As we were leaving the hospital, we met Brent, Melynda and Beth. We took them up to Tim's room for one final goodbye.

Outside the hospital, reporters were still waiting for us. Even they were shocked by the university's and the community's reaction to the tragedy. One was overheard comparing Texas A&M and College Station to Disney World. "It's just too good to be true."

They were referring to the spirit of community and sense of family togetherness that exists at Texas A&M. That spirit and that sense, which had supported our family through this time of tragedy, also helped sustain the rescue workers, university staff, and onlookers at the site and at the hospital. Free food and drinks from grocery stores and restaurants, complimentary hotel rooms for relatives of the victims, offers of rides for families who had flown into town. Anything one could do to help had been done without waiting to be asked.

After discussing the wonderful Aggie family and why Tim, Jr. had chosen Texas A&M, one TV reporter began to preface his next question with "You seem so strong in the face of this tragedy…" at which point I cut him off.

"It's not us," I told him. "It's the Lord Jesus. If it were us talking to you, we'd be a pile of jelly lying here on the floor. We are not strong. The Lord is strong." Some may call that pious talk. But it's not: Only the strength of the Lord can carry people at times like these. If we had not had Him with us, I doubt we would have made it through. All that is needed is to tell Him that we can't do it by ourselves and we need Him. And He will be there. We know from first-hand experience, now.

Later that night in our hotel room, my husband and I agreed that, despite our tremendous grief, we also felt a great sense of peace—"the peace that passes understanding." That doesn't mean we were out of tears. Quite the opposite. By morning my eyes were nearly swollen shut from crying and lack of sleep. I still cry almost every day—some days harder than others. It is a great release, and I don't let crying bother me. Grieving is not only permissible; it's necessary. Although it may be difficult to understand, my husband and I have discovered that God *can* give you peace in the midst of grief if you let Him.

Chapter 3

The Aggie Family Remembers

"We are the Aggies—the Aggies are we,
True to each other as Aggies can be."
The Spirit of Aggieland

The day after Tim died was my husband's birthday. We spent most of it making memorial service arrangements for our son.

Texas A&M had provided rooms at the on-campus Guest Quarters hotel in the Memorial Student Center (MSC) for us and for my husband's children, Michele and Sean. The rooms were extremely nice and very convenient. The university also provided meals, phones, and counselors in a nearby conference room in the MSC.

When we walked into the conference room, we were introduced to Richard and Judy Frampton, whose son, Jeremy, also had died. He and his friend, Jerry Self, had been out celebrating Jerry's promotion to a supervisory "brown pot" position in the Bonfire hierarchy, but both had returned to work shortly before it fell. Having climbed to the fourth level, both were killed instantly. Jeremy was the only other casualty from outside Texas, and his family and fiancée had flown in from California. As we embraced, Judy offered her condolences. "I'm so sorry," she said, "I know it had to be rough knowing that your son was in pain and suffered. At least I know that Jeremy didn't suffer."

What she said was true, but I also knew that she had suffered something I had not. This made me all the sadder for her. "But I got the opportunity to tell my son goodbye," I said. "You didn't have that."

She replied tearfully. "I would have done anything if I could have held him again and told him that I loved him just one more time."

I couldn't help but think about the last time I had held Tim. We couldn't really hold him in the hospital. He was too banged up and the medical equipment made it difficult to get too close. But during our October visit, I held him like I did in the good old days. He was sleeping in the bed next to ours in the hotel room. I had already gotten dressed and his dad was in the shower. I saw Tim sleeping on his side in the bed, and something urged me to lie beside him and "spoon" him for a few minutes. He pretended to sleep through it all, but I knew he felt me snuggle him and put my arms around him. For a few moments, he was my baby again. I also remembered the big hug I gave him just before we left College Station that day. As I reflect on those moments, I think it was the work of the Holy Spirit, enabling us to have those last few intimate moments before the tragedy occurred three weeks later.

Michele, Pete and Sean joined us for breakfast, while I called our pastor, Rick Kirchoff, to tell him about Tim's beautiful, spiritual death experience. We tentatively planned the service for the following Saturday near Memphis. Since that would be Thanksgiving weekend, we knew many of his friends would be home from college, and they would have a chance to say their farewells, too. Reverend Kirchoff was largely unaware of how well-known and popular Tim was in the community or of his many involvements with activities and organizations. So he seemed surprised when I told him that our five hundred and fifty-seat church was not large enough to hold the number of people we anticipated for Tim's service. Since it was a holiday weekend, Rick believed that many people would be out of town and unable to attend the service. He also felt that Tim's service should be held in his home church. I certainly agreed with that, so we discussed using the church's video system for a closed-circuit broadcast of the service to the Family Life Center. I left the final decision on location in his hands.

While we were in the conference room, a member of the Texas A&M Emergency Medical team called and spoke with Sean, who recommended she also speak with Tim, Sr. or me. Since my husband was on another phone with relatives, I took the call. The young medic, Carrie Lunceford, said she'd been one of the first emergency workers to reach Tim after the accident and that she wanted to tell us how brave he was. She said he never cried or complained, although she knew how severe his injuries were and that he must have been in great pain. Carrie said she was crying when she reached Tim, who grabbed her hand so tightly that she feared it would break. She asked Tim if she could pray with him and, of course, Tim agreed. She prayed for God's angels to surround them all. Then Tim prayed for her and the other rescue workers. "He was more of a comfort to me than I was to him," she said. Knowing that one of Tim's last conscious acts was to pray for others was also a great comfort to me, for this further confirmed what I already knew: that the Lord indeed had a special plan for him.

Jim Wheeler arrived just as we were finishing our phone calls. The way Laurinda had been our spiritual guide up to and during Tim's death, Jim Wheeler would now be our caretaker for the next few days. We talked with Jim for a while, and then he took us to the funeral home. Tim, Sr.

and I had decided upon a formal service in College Station for Tim's squadron and other friends; so before leaving the hospital Friday night we made arrangements for a Sunday afternoon service at A&M United Methodist Church.

Many people were surprised at our decision to have Tim's body cremated. They seemed more surprised to learn it had been his request. Earlier that summer, before he left for college, one of our family conversations was interrupted by a telephone call from a cemetery representative selling burial plots. I quickly ended the sales pitch by informing the salesman that we planned to be cremated and, therefore, did not need his services. Assuming Tim, Jr. would be the one to carry out our plans, I proceeded to tell him that after cremation his father and I wanted our ashes spread at Crab Tree Falls in Virginia. We'd been there on a family camping trip several years before, and Tim knew the area. His reply surprised me, because not many people his age ever pause to consider their own mortality. He told me that he also wanted to be cremated, and even knew where to spread his ashes.

"Where is that?" I inquired. "In Glacier National Park?"

"No, in Philmont." Philmont is the National Boy Scout Reservation in New Mexico. I wondered why he would tell me this. Surely, his Dad and I would be gone long before him. In retrospect, though, I believe this conversation was another example of the Holy Spirit working in our lives, preparing us for his untimely death.

This conversation took place before he became an Aggie. But knowing his love for Texas A&M, Tim, Sr. and I decided it would be appropriate to also spread some of his ashes at the eagle fountain on campus, in a small park just across the street from the football stadium. It seemed fitting that our Eagle Scout son, the "Twelfth Man of Bonfire" forever be near Kyle Field, "The Home of the Twelfth Man." We think our decision would have pleased him.

Of course, we knew the ritual was only symbolic. The ashes we spread were not Tim. John 3:6 from *The Message* reads, "When you look at a baby, it's just that: a body you can look at and touch. But the person who takes shape within is formed by something you can't see and touch—the Spirit—and becomes a living spirit." Tim's spirit, his true self, could never be contained in a body. And it lives on, in all who knew him, for as long as they live.

Tim had been an active member of our church drama group, ACTS (Acting for Christ through Theater and Song). During his junior year of high school, Tim performed a monologue from *Lenten Voices* as Nicodemus, the Pharisee who sought out Jesus by night to ask him theological questions. The verse above, John 3:6, is a portion of the conversation between Jesus and Nicodemus. Tim's monologue takes place immediately after the Crucifixion and opens with Nicodemus kneeling at the foot of the cross. He stands and repeats Jesus' last statement: "Father, into your hands, I commit my spirit." Nicodemus then tells about his secret meeting with Jesus and their discussion, and ends the soliloquy with the resultant change in his beliefs. "Since then, I have never stopped longing to be a servant in His kingdom. But now I know it means more than feeding the poor, more than prophesying, even more than faith. It means surrendering my spirit to Him…Father, into your hands I commit *my* spirit."

Although Tim's masterful performance moved many in the congregation to tears, for him it was not an act. More important than his beautiful recitation of the words was the fact that he *had* committed his spirit to God. The knowledge that his spirit belonged to God and continued living in those who'd known him made the physical loss of Tim easier to accept. It really didn't matter to us if he were buried or cremated—that crushed body was not my son.

After completing our business at the funeral home, Jim Wheeler, my husband, and I talked about details of the memorial service that would involve the cadets. Did we want to have members of the Singing Cadets vocal group perform? If so, what songs would we like? A cadet had offered to play "Amazing Grace" on the bagpipes—were we interested? Did we have a picture to display at the memorial service? Did we want a bugler to blow "Taps"? We expressed our wishes to Jim, and he left to take care of the details, including having some of Tim's buddies begin packing his personal effects. He left the job of polishing Tim's boots to the fish in his squadron. That turned out to be good therapy, especially for Widodo. He must have used eight coats of polish on those boots, so bright did they shine. Jim's presence to tend to these matters was yet another blessing. We were in such a fog; I doubt Tim, Sr. and I could have handled everything.

While Jim handled those affairs, Tim, Sr. and I met with Rev. Charles Anderson and Laurinda. Reverend Anderson had been to see us at St. Joseph's Hospital, stopping by when he could while ministering to other injured and grieving students and their families. Laurinda had stayed with us through most of the hospital experience, except for Thursday evening. We discussed the music to be used, the order of the service, and—most important to us— the fact that this service was to be a celebration of Tim's life.

While we were at the church, a young couple came in for their final pre-marital counseling session with the pastor. We were told that the groom-to-be was offering to give us his Aggie ring for our son. To loyal Aggies, the gold class ring is more precious than the diploma. It symbolizes everything meaningful to them about Texas A&M—the traditions, pride, loyalty, and values that the students hold so dear and make the university a unique place. Even after less than two months on campus, Tim had already calculated how many credits he would have to take each semester in order to get his ring as soon as possible! My husband and I were moved to disbelief by the offer. Deeply touched, we told the young man to keep his ring and wear it in Tim's memory.

After leaving the church, we stopped by the squadron dorm to check on the kids. I had urged the fish not to let Widodo spend the night alone, and I wanted to follow up on the request. Lucky Widodo! The female cadets in the squadron were looking after him like mother hens. One had slept the night on the floor in his hole. Out of respect for Tim, she would not sleep in his rack. Beth and Melynda spent the night in that dorm as well, and many of the students had stayed up late sharing more Tim stories. As Tim's "old lady," they said Widodo had a lot of tales to tell. Of all Tim's belongings, we opted to leave behind his bicycle for use by any member of the squadron who needed to use it.

True to form, our offer reminded someone of yet another Tim story— this one by fish (Emily) Porterfield. Both she and Tim were in the honors program, which entitled them to register for classes before non-honors students. They stayed up until midnight so they could be online to register at the earliest possible minute. Both encountered problems registering, and they ran to the computer center to fix the bugs. They returned to the dorm and tried again, still with no luck. Emily got a head start leaving for the computer center, trying to beat him to the punch. "I was so happy," she remembers thinking on the run across campus. "I thought that at last I was going to beat Kerlee at something. I was jogging along, and I heard a noise. Here came Kerlee on his bicycle pedaling past me, and he just looked over his shoulder and started grinning at me! He beat me again!"

That afternoon, we also made the trek across campus to the Bonfire site, which was located on the Polo Field, adjacent to the university's main entrance. I was completely unprepared for the sight that met us. Hanging between the trees alongside the Polo Field were huge banners expressing support from rival Big 12 Conference schools such as Baylor and UT. Hundreds of people walked around, many crying and consoling each other. An orange plastic mesh construction fence surrounded the huge piles of logs that just days earlier had been the nearly completed bonfire stack, and half of the fence was covered with flowers, poems, posters, and Aggie shirts, hats and other memorabilia. Hardly a bare spot could be found. "Twelfth Man" towels hung on the fence; signs that had read "to our 11 fallen Aggies" had been changed to read " to our 12 fallen Aggies." A student had left his Aggie ring at the flagpole, with a note explaining that since most of the victims would never get to wear an Aggie Ring, he would leave them his for a while. He would be back later to pick it up. This inspired others and eventually, more than a dozen rings were left at the flagpole.

This gesture was doubly inspiring. Not only did it speak to the powerful bond between Aggies that one would leave his ring as a gesture of solidarity with the fallen, but also to the sense of security that such a bond inspires. Where else could one feel the confidence that a solid-gold ring left unattended would still be there after several days? They may be solid gold, but the worth of an Aggie Ring is not measured in dollars.

We spoke with many students who told us that no one had gone to class on Thursday or Friday. Although classes were not officially canceled, professors postponed scheduled exams and those students who ventured to class more often than not found them empty. The entire campus and community was in a collective state of shock. By Thursday afternoon, we learned, thousands of students had gathered in the plaza by Rudder Fountain adjacent to the Memorial Students Center. Dazed and disbelieving, they sat, cried, and prayed for hours. Student Body President Will Hurd had arranged a formal memorial service for Thursday evening in Reed Arena, the campus basketball venue. The 12,000-plus-seat arena was packed with mourners. At the time of the service, eight had been confirmed dead and anxious parents hoped against hope that their children would be found alive in the pile of fallen logs. Sadly, that was not to be the case. Late Thursday evening, the last three bodies were uncovered.

My husband and I were at the hospital during the Reed Arena service, but have since watched it on videotape. It was an honorable tribute to the deceased and injured, but I think what happened after the ceremony was officially over says a great deal about Texas A&M. The University of Texas' student body president, Eric Opiela, attended the service and later wrote this letter about it:

> The A&M student body is truly one of the great treasures of our state. As part of the UT delegation, we sat on the floor of Reed Arena and immediately following the end of the service, I heard this rustling sound behind me.

I looked over my shoulder and saw the sight of close to 20,000 students spontaneously putting their arms on their neighbor's shoulders, forming a great circle around the arena.

The mass stood there in pin-drop silence for close to five minutes, then, from somewhere, someone began to hum quietly the hymn, *Amazing Grace*. Within seconds, the whole arena was singing.

I tried, too—I choked; I cried. This event brought me to tears. It was one of—if not the—defining moment of my college career. I learned something tonight. For all us Longhorns to discount A&M in our never-ending rivalry, we need to realize one thing. Aggieland is a special place, with special people.

It is infinitely better equipped than we are at dealing with a tragedy such as this for one simple reason. It is a family. It is a family that cares for its own; a family that reaches out; a family that is unified in the face of adversity; a family that moved this Longhorn to tears.

My heart, my prayers, and the heart of the UT student body go out tonight to Aggies and their families and friends as they recover from this great loss. Texas A&M, The Eyes of Texas are Upon You—and they look with sincere sympathy upon a family that has been through so much tragedy this semester.

There is an expression at Texas A&M about the loyalty and sense of family that most Aggies feel toward each other. "From the outside looking in, you can't understand it; and from the inside looking out, you can't explain it." This letter shows that at least one "outsider" understands it now. There is another expression: "Once an Aggie—Always an Aggie." The students who have attended Texas A&M are called "former students." There is no such thing as a former Aggie. The sense of belonging to something bigger than oneself knows no generation gap. As we walked around the Bonfire site that day, we saw current students, former students, and future students. Each of them had been cut to the core with a great sense of loss. To them, they had lost ten brothers and two sisters.

Twelve young people died while working on a project that many of them had worked on in the past or hoped to work on the future—a project that was more than just building a huge fire. Aggie Bonfire also built camaraderie and teamwork, developed leadership skills, promoted school spirit and symbolized Texas A&M's unity. Aggies everywhere were in deep mourning for their lost "family members."

Our family had dinner that Saturday evening at the home of Jim and Pam Reynolds. Jim Reynolds is the director of the MSC and a personal friend of Jim Wheeler. I remembered him from New Student Orientation Week, which includes sessions for parents as well as incoming students. During one of the parent sessions I attended, Jim spoke about moral and spiritual values. I was pleased and impressed by his views on the subject, and about Texas A&M's approach to them.

He said that many universities want their students to come to them with an open mind about their sense of values, and the faculty tries to wipe out everything they have been taught in this regard. Jim told us that, "We know that you have worked for eighteen years to instill your values and morals in your child. We don't want to erase that. We try to encourage them to keep those values and experience spiritual growth as well as academic growth." I knew right then that Texas A&M was the right school for Tim.

Jim Wheeler had told Jim and Pam Reynolds that it was my husband's birthday, so we had birthday cake, and they and the Wheelers gave Tim, Sr. a Texas A&M windbreaker as a birthday present. They also gave me an A&M sweatshirt. This was yet another of the so many different ways that someone at Texas A&M or in College Station had tried to relieve some of the pain and ease the burden of our shared sorrow.

Many of our friends in Memphis later told us how bad they felt because we were so far from home during that terrible time. "You didn't have any family or friends to support you," they said. I always smiled as I gently corrected them. We were surrounded the entire time by friends, enveloped by the love of our new Aggie family.

The old expression was right. "From the outside looking in, you can't understand it, and from the inside looking out, you can't explain it." Only now was I beginning to understand it. Being an Aggie was in many ways like being a Christian. Until you accept Christ in your heart and become a part of the Christian family, you can't really understand it. To someone who doesn't have the Holy Spirit in their life, it all seems a bit ludicrous. And as much as a Christian may try to explain to someone else what it is like, words just can't do it justice. Being a Christian is something that has to be experienced. It's a similar feeling for an Aggie. You are a part of a loving family. You may have differences, but you will always be there for each other. The long lasting traditions give all Aggies common experiences, and the school spirit is so strong that you feel bound in a way to everyone who has ever been a part of the University. But to truly understand the Aggie family, you need to experience it.

Chapter 4

The Twelfth Man

"Greater love hath no man than this;
that a man lay down his life for his friends."
John 15:13 (*KJV*)

Sunday morning, my husband and I attended a special remembrance and prayer service at A&M United Methodist Church. It was one of many such services held throughout the area for those who'd been killed or injured in Thursday's collapse. Tim's memorial would be held here later in the day.

So many times in the past two days we'd heard about Tim's leadership from others. At A&M United Methodist, however, he'd signed up for the church's program that pairs students with adult mentors. When we discussed this with Beth, she told us he had many mentors. "He had a mentor for everything," she said. "One time he said he was meeting with his mentor and I asked him, 'Which one? You have more mentors than anybody I've ever known!'"

Bob and Margaret Appleton had bonded quickly with Tim, who sat with them at church. Bob even attended a squadron "father-son cut" barbecue with Tim because it was too far for my husband to travel. That had really meant a great deal to Tim and to us.

Appreciative of their interest in our son and aware of the pain they, too, were suffering at his loss, we asked the Appletons to sit with us at the morning service. We also invited them to join us for brunch and to be at our side that afternoon for Tim's service. Their service as spiritual guides for our son, who was so far from home, also forged a bond between them and us, and I was thankful to have them close that day.

During the morning service, the emotional enormity overwhelmed me; I dropped to my knees in prayer and tears. I believe the cleansing tears and release helped prepare me for the afternoon, allowing me to make it through Tim's service without breaking down.

Entering the church before the afternoon service, I saw a young man in a wheelchair being helped out of a van. I stopped, then walked over and introduced myself to him. A lump rose to my throat when I learned he was Derek Woodley, who'd changed places with Tim on the swing shortly before the collapse. Having already encountered survivor's guilt in Widodo and several other young people in the previous two days, I knew that Derek likely would be haunted by the memory of what had happened and blurted out, "Don't you dare have survivor guilt. Why should your parents be suffering and grieving instead of us? Just thank God that you are okay."

Later, his father told us that he had tried to convince Derek to stay home and rest because of his injuries. Derek insisted on going to Tim's Memorial Service, and his father had to relent.

Inside the church, eleven candles had been placed on the altar in tribute to the other fallen Aggies. On a table in front of the sanctuary stood a twelfth candle, beside a photograph of Tim. Also there were his senior boots, campaign hat and saber. The walls were adorned with flowers.

Along with the Appletons, we had invited Jim Wheeler and several of Tim's friends to sit with us at the service. Only later did I realize that our "family" group totaled eleven. Once again, Tim was the Twelfth Man.

Four members of the Singing Cadets opened the service by singing "The Twelfth Man." After some scripture and words of greeting, the congregation sang the hymn "Heaven Came Down." After another prayer, Laurinda read the Twenty-third Psalm, which was, of course, a Song of David. This was followed by a rendition of "Joyful, Joyful, We Adore Thee" by the Singing Cadets. Then Laurinda spoke some words of remembrance.

She spoke of Tim's joy and zest for life. Over and over, she had heard from his friends about his ever-present smile, with its small gap between the front teeth that made it so special. Hearing this, I recalled how I'd tried to convince him to have the teeth bonded after his braces were removed, to keep them from separating again. He wouldn't hear of it. Doing that would prevent him from making funny robot like sounds, or squirting water between his teeth. His appearance simply was not as important to him as the ability to have a good time—and to make sure others did, too.

"His friends talk about how much fun it was to be around Tim," Laurinda said. "If he was with you, he was either helping you or making you laugh." She asked the congregation:

How many of us take the time to love life as much as Tim did? How many of us will be more intentional about that now that we have known and loved Tim? Because, you see, Tim Kerlee affected more people in his seventeen years of life than most people do in seventy. In fact, I believe that it is safe to say that he affected more people in the last four months, than many of us do in four decades.

What I learned about Tim Kerlee was that to know him was to love him. If you knew Tim, you liked Tim. He was accepting of all people. He had no prejudice; he accepted you for who you were. He never did anything halfway. He always gave a hundred-and-ten percent…Our most precious memories today are the ones that showed us how Tim gave a hundred and ten percent to God…

I believe that when we die a part of us stays with the people we leave behind. Something about us stays and it lives in the people who know and love us. What is it about Tim that will stay with you? Let it be that love for life; make it a burning desire to know and love God.

I was infused with peace as I listened to her soothing voice and inspirational words. It was not the first time in those few days that Laurinda's words had brought me comfort and inspiration—far from it! She and I had shared many stories about Tim at his hospital bedside, and these provided much of the material for her eulogy. I knew that she had come to see and admire in my son many of the same qualities that made him so dear to me.

Once, Laurinda shared with him a remark I had made to her while he was sleeping. "Tim, your mom tells me that if there is an easy way to do something and a hard way to do it, but the hard way is fun, that you will always pick the hard, fun way." Tim smiled at this.

I smiled, too. I thought back to an assignment he'd had in the sixth grade. He had to describe his favorite character from Mark Twain's "Huckleberry Finn" and explain why he'd chosen that character. Tim chose Huck because he was so much like him: both always found a way to turn challenges into fun. "I see a lot of myself in Huck," he had written.

After Laurinda's eulogy, two cadets played "Amazing Grace" on the bagpipes. Then Mike Lightfoot, the church's music director, played the guitar and sang a song about David, "A Man after God's Own Heart."

Reverend Anderson's sermon, based on Paul's letters to the Philippians, offered us hope. In Chapter 1, Paul wrote: "I thank my God every time I remember you, constantly praying with joy in every one of my prayers for all of you, because of your sharing in the gospel from the first day until now. And I am confident of this, that the one who began a good work among you will bring it to completion by the day of Jesus Christ."

His sermon encouraged sharing memories as a way to heal. He discussed the pain caused by unfinished business, and offered hope by reminding us that God leaves no task incomplete. "When God begins a good work like Tim, then God completes it," he said. "Life can't stop Him, time can't stop Him, death can't stop Him, tears can't stop Him. God leaves no unfinished business."

He urged us to give Tim to God, along with any of our unfinished business with Tim. Thankfully, neither my husband nor I had any unfinished business with our son. Our relationship, so open and complete, was one that made it easy to deal with anything then and there, and move beyond it. Our presence during his final hours, and our active sharing of his beautiful, spiritual death experience, guaranteed that no loose ends remained.

Unfinished business with our son may have troubled others before hearing the reverend's words, but they only reinforced my sense of peace. The preceding days had brought me so many new insights into the true meaning of scriptures, and now I truly understood the proverb, "Don't let the sun set upon your wrath."

This doesn't mean we have to agree with our loved ones on everything. We will always have our differences. What is important is that we never allow an unresolved conflict to divide us. We never know what life holds. If we part from a loved one in anger, and something happens to them, would they die knowing we loved them? Or would we forever be haunted by guilt and feel the pain of unfinished business?

God had begun in Tim a good work, Reverend Anderson said, and he would see it through to completion. "How wonderful to know that God is not finished with Tim yet," he said. Certainly God had not been finished with Tim while he was dying.

Tim, Sr. and I knew that our son loved the Lord and lived his life serving Him, and we have come to realize that even imminent death could not stand in the way of his glorifying God. Knowing Tim, I suppose I should have known that God would use him in a special way. Just how special, however, I did not know until after the service when several young people who'd been at the collapse shared with us the story of his exceptional courage while trapped in the fallen stack.

According to several witnesses, Tim kept insisting to rescue workers that he was okay. He urged them to first tend to his buddies—even pointing out to them five others who were trapped and in need of help. He was also concerned about Derek Woodley, who was lying on the ground with a broken arm, broken leg and several compressed vertebrae. Tim continually shouted to Derek, asking if he was all right and trying to prompt a response from his semi-conscious buddy. Derek doesn't remember any of this. Only after the five trapped victims were freed from the debris did Tim allow the rescuers to begin work freeing him. Truly, he exemplified the Spirit of the Twelfth Man.

Immediately after he died, I asked God, "Why did you wake me up and tell me to pray for Tim, and them let him die?" Then I realized that God had answered my prayer, just not in the way I had expected. With the severity of his injuries, Tim never should have made it to the hospital alive. But God kept him alive to pray with Carrie, to send the rescuers to his buddies, and to allow us to be with him. He had almost died three times on the operating table, yet the Lord gave us a chance to say goodbye—to be there for his beautiful death experience. Tim left for heaven knowing how much he was loved and admired, and he knew how he had made a difference in the lives of those around him. The presence of God we felt in that hospital room reassured us that he was in the best of hands.

After Reverend Anderson's sermon, buglers from the Corps played "Taps," prayers were said, and our family and close friends left the sanctuary with everyone singing, "On Eagles' Wings." Each uniformed cadet walked to the front of the sanctuary to deliver a sharp salute to Tim's picture, then did a quick about-face, and exited after the family. With them was Derek Woodley, in his wheelchair and wearing civilian clothing because his injuries prevented him from being in uniform. Derek later approached me and said, "I'm going to make you proud, ma'am." I managed only a tearful hug in reply.

More than 650 people attended Tim's memorial, many of whom had known him personally. Others where there to honor a fallen Aggie brother, such as the Air Force officer who flew from South Carolina because, like Tim, he had served in the Corps' Falcon 16 squadron. Also in attendance was Margaret Rudder, widow of General Earl Rudder, a hero of Normandy who later served as president of Texas A&M. Mrs. Rudder said she had read and heard so many good things about Tim that she wanted to join in honoring him. She said she could tell that he was well respected. An elderly gentleman from Austin with no connection to the university also told us he had come to pay tribute to our son after reading about him in the paper.

We spent more than an hour in the church's courtyard speaking with those who had come to memorialize and honor our son. As we were about to leave, I was summoned to the church office to take a phone call. It was my cousin Steven Dorner, whom I hadn't seen since he left for Vietnam. Cousin Steve had not been drafted, but believing that God wanted him to care for those injured in combat, he volunteered and became a medic. He later married a Texan and settled in San Antonio. After more than thirty years, I had forgotten that I had a cousin in Texas. He apologized for not having called sooner but said he didn't recognize my married name, nor did he know I had a son at Texas A&M.

What he told me next sent a chill down my spine: A salesman, he had been in College Station and staying in a hotel across the street from the Bonfire site when it fell. He wanted to come to College Station to spend the next day with us and we arranged to meet on Monday. Then the family and I returned to the MSC Guest Quarters to freshen up for dinner.

After dinner, we went to the Corps dorms for "Echo Taps," a brief ceremony held whenever a fellow cadet has died. That week, they had lost eight, making it a particularly solemn occasion. The entire Corps assembled by units along both sides of the Quadrangle, the central courtyard in the Corps' dorm area. Three notes at a time, a lone bugler slowly sounded "Taps" at one end of the Quad, echoed by another lone bugler at the opposite end. I shivered with emotion at the mournful, yet peaceful and touching ceremony. I had never been a big fan of ceremony, yet this instilled in me a sense of pride and loyalty in the face of tremendous loss. At Texas A&M especially, ceremony and tradition are central to the continuity that binds Aggies forever—even after death. Our son Sean also was moved by the experience, later expressing the hope that his own children would someday attend Texas A&M. The units were dismissed and quietly marched back into their dorms. Many returned to the Quad to again offer their condolences before we left.

Michele, Pete and Sean left for home early the following morning. Tim, Sr. and I had a lot of loose ends to tie up before leaving College Station, and we were meeting Laurinda and my cousin Steve for lunch. Together, we then went back to the Bonfire site. Another large crowd was present outside the orange security fence, to which had been added even more poems, flowers and other mementos. A large wooden cross had been brought to the site, around which most of the people were gathered. Across the horizontal beam was written a verse from scripture: "Greater love hath no man than this, that a man lay down his life for his friends."

People were signing the cross and adding words of condolence. So many had signed the cross that there was no room left for any more messages. A sheet of plywood was set up next to the cross, to allow more expressions of sorrow and support. Nearby were twelve smaller white crosses—one for each victim, with their names written on them in maroon, maroon and white being Texas A&M's school colors. Personal friends had left special messages and mementos around the crosses.

Reading the messages left at Tim's cross reminded us of the depth of our shared loss, and Steve, Tim, Sr. and I decided to have dinner that evening with the fish from Squadron 16. We needed each other's company and opted to eat at the dining hall rather than a restaurant. Attendance was sparse. Many students still could not bring themselves to go to class and had left early for the Thanksgiving break. Others were on their way to Austin, for a joint vigil with students from rival UT. The school had opted to replace its annual "hex rally," at which red candles were traditionally burned on a night before the football game, with a white-candle "unity vigil" in honor of the fallen Aggies. This year, the traditional rivalry had been set aside and students from Texas A&M were invited to participate— a tremendous show of support by the university and its students.

Less than three months into the 1999–2000 school year, the bonfire collapse marked the third tragedy to strike Texas A&M. Five died in a crash of the skydiving club's plane, and one Aggie and five other students walking along a College Station road were killed when they were struck by a pickup truck whose driver—a Texas A&M freshman—had fallen asleep. Now, twelve Aggies had died participating in one of Texas A&M's most cherished traditions. The sad cloud hanging over the College Station campus served to put Friday's football match-up in its proper perspective. It was only a game. This was real life.

Chapter 5

Carpe Diem

"Listen, you hear it?…Hear it?…
Carpe, carpe diem, seize the day boys;
make your lives extraordinary."
Dead Poets Society

We flew back to Memphis on Tuesday, November 23. Our best friends, Don and Rory Theeuwes, and Jim Eddy, a fellow Scouter, met us at the airport. As we turned the corner onto our street, I saw every mailbox on the block adorned with a white or maroon ribbon—alternating colors as we passed them. I later learned that our neighbors, Dennis and Joanne Cain and their children, Heather and Matt, had arranged this show of support and solidarity. Several men from our Sunday School class had tended to our home in our absence, weeding the garden and raking the yard, and even planting flowers. They felt our place should look more welcoming for the many visitors they knew we'd be receiving after our return.

I also learned that when several women from the church had come over offering to clean house for us, they found those chores already being attended to by our neighbor Maxi Paganonni and Jennifer Dyer, who was house sitting. Friends and neighbors had already brought food and disposable serving ware, and Libby Scheilke, also in our Sunday School class, was arranging for food for the reception that would follow Tim's memorial. Tracy Clarke, a member of the local Aggie club, had arranged for free hotel rooms for out of town family and friends who would be coming for Saturday's service.

A Memphis funeral home had donated pens and registry books. Flowers and plants adorned the interior of the house; and friends had made small maroon and white ribbons to wear at the memorial service. Other friends offered to pick up our out of town relatives at the airport. My colleague and good friend Berta Nance came to the house to answer the phone and door, and record the many gifts of flowers and food. Once again, people were doing anything they could think of to show their love and sympathy. God was truly good to give us such thoughtful friends!

Appreciative though I was, it was at first difficult for me to accept their offers of assistance. Normally, I try to do for others—it's not my nature to be a "taker." I quickly got over this, though, evidenced in the way I delegated duties! The adjustment was made easier by the realization that it truly is more blessed to give than to receive, and that by trying to handle everything myself I would be denying those blessings to my many wonderful friends. Besides, I never could have managed it all single-handedly.

The outpouring of assistance made me think of the story of the man who was warned of a coming flood by the sheriff, who offered him a ride to safety. The man responded, "I'll be OK, God will save me." The flood arrived and he took refuge in a tree, later refusing help from a group of men in a rowboat below. "No," he insisted, "God is looking out for me.

He will save me." The waters continued rising and the man made his way to a rooftop. A helicopter soon arrived and, again, the man refused rescue. "I'm a good Christian," he said. "God will save me." The flood swept the house away and the man drowned. He arrived in Heaven a bit confused and unhappy with God, and promptly questioned the Lord on failing to provide for his safety. God simply answered, "I sent you a car, a boat, and a helicopter. What else did you want?"

Fortunately for us, as the floodwaters steadily rose around us, the Lord sent us a small fleet of life rafts in the form of friends. And we had the good sense to climb aboard them, and thus keep our heads above the sea of sorrow that otherwise would have drowned us. The many arrangements that needed to be made, and other details to attend to, surely would have washed over us if not for them. Even with the outpouring of assistance, at times I felt there should be three of me to handle arrangements for the memorial service, interviews with reporters, telephone calls and visits with family and friends, and many other tasks and responsibilities.

When our pastor, Rick Kirchoff, came by to discuss the service, Tim, Sr. and I found it hard to find even fifteen minutes of peace and quiet to tend to this. Despite the many interruptions, Rick did an excellent job pulling together our scattered thoughts and shaping them into a very meaningful service. Among the many things we'd planned to do was sort through our many pictures and videos of Tim, for use in a memorial video being produced by Steven Marinos, a fifteen-year-old member of our church; the video was to be shown at the reception following Saturday's memorial. Steven dedicated himself fully to the task at hand, knowing how much it meant to us. Beginning on Wednesday evening and working through Thanksgiving Day and most of Friday, he had it complete in time for Tim, Sr. and I to review on Friday evening.

Steven had done an excellent job, using still photos in a "slide show" set to music, and interspersed with video clips of Tim's Eagle Scout ceremony and scenes from his various stage performances. He ended with Tim's moving and inspirational Nicodemus monologue from *Lenten Voices*.

Truly a labor of love, yet Steven's work was not yet finished. After giving up his Thanksgiving holidays for the project, he also agreed to videotape the memorial service and provide the video feed to three networks. With TV professionals by his side offering suggestions on which shots to get, he managed a nearly flawless job. I say "nearly flawless" only because of a three-second interruption caused when one of the network pros accidentally flipped a switch at his elbow!

We spent Thanksgiving at the home of Ben and Mary Ellen Kemker, friends of ours from Scouting and members of our church. Mary Ellen also had been Tim's Explorer adviser. Although it was good to be with caring friends, it didn't feel much like Thanksgiving. I suppose it will be a long time before we can really celebrate that holiday. It's not that we don't have a lot to be thankful for. We are grateful for the time that God had given Timothy to be with us, for Timothy's personal relationship with Jesus Christ, and for having been able to serve as midwives for his spiritual birth. We are thankful to have a strong marriage and each other to rely on. I can't imagine going through this ordeal without my soul mate, Tim, Sr. The loss of a child puts a tremendous strain on a marriage, and I've since heard that many end in divorce within one year of a child's death. These are couples whom the stress pulls apart, rather than drawing together.

But Tim, Sr. and I are most grateful for the loving God who has carried us so much of the time since the loss of Tim. I truly know the Lord has carried us because so many things have happened that I simply don't remember. Major events stand out, but so many details are lost to me. I'm told this is common when dealing with a great deal of stress. For so much of this time, God served as an automatic pilot for my life. He has flown the plane, while I was but a passenger along for the ride. I know that without His strength, my husband and I would not have made it this far. My own strength was not sufficient to carry me through. When I still was teaching classes, for example, I would be fine. Perhaps focusing on the day's lessons helped keep my emotions in check and my mind clear. But the end of the school day frequently found me again in tears. I know that our hearts will be forever scarred, but am given hope by the knowledge that scarring is a sign of healing. In this case, it is evidence of God working to mend our broken lives. It is therefore for his unending love and patience that we are most grateful.

So although that Thursday didn't feel much like Thanksgiving, and the memories of that week will forever change the feeling of both Thanksgiving and my husband's birthday, we did have—and continue to have—much to be grateful for.

While we were busy making plans for Saturday, thousands of people continued streaming into College Station. There was no Bonfire that Thursday night as planned, but the Aggie Spirit nonetheless burned bright at a candlelight vigil held on the bonfire site. The university had planned nothing, other than providing more than 80,000 maroon and white candles for the anticipated crowd. This was a purposeful decision to allow events to unfold naturally. The vigil was a solemn occasion, with many people crying and praying. At one point, a man in a cowboy hat and boots carried an Aggie flag at half-staff and walked the perimeter of the field. As he passed, attendees raised their candles to him in silent salute. A lone bugler played, "How Great thou Art." After the vigil, the Fightin' Texas Aggie Band led the crowd in a march to the football stadium, Kyle Field, for a modified "Yell Practice."

Unlike most other colleges, Texas A&M doesn't have cheers. They have "yells" which, along with the school song, "The Spirit of Aggieland," and the fight song, "The Aggie War Hymn" are taught to incoming students at Fish Camp. Consequently, Aggies don't have pep rallies; they have Yell Practice. At midnight before each football game, at home or on the road, Aggies gather to rehearse their "yells" for the next day's game. Midnight Yell Practice always follows Bonfire, with the school's (male) "yell leaders" getting tens of thousands of Aggie faithful geared up to urge Texas A&M to "beat the hell out of t.u."

"Beat the hell out of t.u." is a yell reserved for the Thanksgiving game against the Longhorns. This year, however, there would be no such animosity displayed toward the university that had supported the Aggies in their darkest hour. Although that year's Midnight Yell was marked by the same enthusiasm, the overall mood was somewhat subdued. Head Yell Leader Jeff Bailey set the tone with his solemn recitation of the poem, "The Last Corps Trip," which tells of cadets marching through the Gates of Paradise behind the Aggie Band, which leads the Corps march (or "trip") into Kyle Field before each home game. In addition to being recited each year at Bonfire, the poem also is part of Muster, the annual memorial ceremony held each April 21 (Texas Independence Day) for Aggies who've died in the previous year. With eight of the twelve dead connected to the Corps, including one graduate, the poem held special significance this year.

As Yell Practice concluded, the candles were extinguished and a videotape of a previous year's Bonfire was played on the stadium's large-screen TV as a series of twelve cannon volleys was fired in salute to the twelve fallen Aggies. Despite the mournful atmosphere, the burning desire to "beat the hell out of t.u." was as strong as ever.

Shortly after ten the next morning, the nationally televised game kicked off before a crowd of 86,128, at the time the largest audience ever for a football game in Texas. Many of the Longhorn faithful present had pinned small maroon and white ribbons to their burnt-orange clothing in a display of solidarity with their grieving rivals. Within the opening minute, Texas went in front and took a 16-6 lead into the locker room at halftime.

For the halftime performance by the Longhorn Band—"The Show Band of the Southwest"—several members of the flag corps carried Texas A&M flags, yet another unprecedented display by the school for an opponent. The band also cut its performance short, marching off the field after playing "Amazing Grace." I've heard it said (and would rather believe it than learn that the rumor is untrue) that Longhorn Band members were so upset by the tragedy that had befallen their fellow Texas school that, at their final practice before Thanksgiving, they filed off the field one by one after only fifteen minutes.

The military style Fightin' Texas Aggie Band turned in another performance that was awe-inspiring in its crispness and precision, ending their routine with a "silent T" march off the field.

Neither team put any points on the board in the third quarter, but two fourth-quarter touchdowns and a game sealing fumble recovery by freshman linebacker Brian Gamble gave the Aggies a much needed upset victory. "I know God and those twelve angels were looking down on us today, and they helped us to play to the best of our abilities," Gamble would say after the game. Now, I don't believe God cares one way or another about football. But in many ways this was much more than a ball game and so, perhaps there was a touch of divine intervention, designed to help soothe the sorely aching Aggie spirit. The come from behind victory in their final regular-season game certainly provided Aggies everywhere a tremendous boost.

Although it helped lift our sagging spirits somewhat, neither my husband nor I could pay much attention to the game while it was being played. Friends and family from across the country—California, Kentucky, Michigan, Virginia, South Carolina and Florida—were arriving for the memorial service, and our house was rapidly filling with people—and love. Many who came were senior citizens, and the long two-day drive from Virginia had to be very difficult for them. I only wish it could have been for a happy occasion instead of such a sad one. Yet again, I thought back to my mother, who frequently remarked that she didn't want people coming to her funeral. "I'd much rather they come visit me while I'm alive," she would say.

Of course, people who go to funerals aren't there for those who have passed away; they go to provide emotional support to the living. Although I was overwhelmed that so many had come to support Tim and me in our time of need, I also understand my mother's point. Far too often, we unintentionally neglect people when things are going well. Yet, sharing our joy is just as important as sharing sorrow, and I have since committed myself to making more of an effort to be with my loved ones for the good times.

Memories of good times with my friends and family will help sustain me when they are gone, just as those of our happy years with Timothy have since his death. And his memorial service that afternoon would provide a way to preserve and share those good memories with others who knew and loved him, and hopefully this would help sustain them.

Mementos of his life adorned the front of the church. His senior boots and saber, high school letter jacket, class ring, diploma, Bible, Boy Scout uniform shirt—complete with his Eagle pin, merit badge sash, and Explorer Gold Award—all these were there amid the floral arrangements. On the altar burned eleven candles, each one lit by a different member of the Mid-South Aggie Club. The twelfth candle was placed by itself on the right of the altar and stood beside a picture of Tim. It remained unlit at the beginning of the service.

I had been right about our church's ability to handle the crowd for Tim's memorial. Yet even I was astonished at the number who came. Church employees had run video lines to the chapel, fellowship hall and choir room, accommodating more than a thousand people. Still, we were crowded. People stood in the narthex of the church, and lined the sides of the chapel and fellowship hall. In all, ushers counted more than thirteen hundred attendees.

After a greeting by Assistant Pastor Deb Christiansen, prayers and a reading from scripture, we sang several hymns. Among them was "The Hymn of Promise," a powerful song that conveys to us the fact that we cannot see what lies ahead for us on the road of life. That remains a mystery to all but God, and what seems to us a tragedy when it happens may end beautifully. My favorite verses are the first and the last:

> In the bulb there is a flower; in the seed, an apple tree;
> In cocoons, a hidden promise: butterflies will soon be free!
> In the cold and snow of winter there's a spring that waits to be,
> Unrevealed until its season, something God alone can see.

> In our end is our beginning; in our time, infinity;

In our doubt there is believing: in our life eternity.
In our death, a resurrection; at the last, a victory,
Unrevealed until its season, something God alone can see.

We followed the hymns with testimonies to Tim's life and faith. Rick began by speaking of the people who'd influenced Tim's life: his parents, Sunday school teachers, Scout leaders, church youth workers, and school teachers. He discussed the importance of good training and of the positive role models who had helped shape our son's character. The scouts in the audience stood and recited the Scout Law and Oath, representing that influence on his life. Members of ACTS, the church's dramatic group to which Tim had belonged, began their presentation by reciting a poem that defines success:

> To laugh often and much;
> To win the respect of intelligent people and the affection of children;
> To appreciate beauty;
> To find the best in others;
> To leave the world a bit better;
> To know that even one life has breathed easier because you have lived—
> This is to have succeeded.

Stephen Sparks, a member of the group, opened his comments by characterizing the service as a celebration of "the life of a successful person—our friend, Tim Kerlee."

"Tim was his own person. He wasn't afraid to be himself. Whether it was walking into ACTS and announcing, 'I'm here!' or swing dancing when nobody really knew what that was, or being a flowing river for a youth fellowship skit, Tim made every circumstance good," Stephen said. "He made circumstances suit him. He was never afraid to be who he was. I think that's what made him a leader, and why everyone respected him."

His comments were right on target. Months later, I received a letter that Tim had written to himself at the end of Fish Camp, which was then collected by the counselors to be mailed to him at the end of the semester. "Remember to keep your head up and take everything in stride," Tim wrote, "because even though many of the situations you are in were not your choice, how you react to them is your choice and no one else's."

Matt Rhoads and Julie Field, who recounted a line of his from Gilbert and Sullivan's *Pirates of Penzance,* offered further insight into Tim's values. Although intended as humorous, Matt and Julie had concluded that it really defined Tim's outlook on life after hearing him deliver it. "You have appealed to my sense of duty. It is all too clear! Duty comes first…at any price, I will do my duty." What stronger sign of Tim's sense of duty could one need than his actions while trapped in that fallen log pile, refusing aid until his buddies had been seen to? Duty demanded they be taken care of first!

His memorable role as Nicodemus was recalled by Steven Solomon and Will Goodwin, in particular the line, "The other Pharisees would say of me: Nicodemus is never satisfied—and it was true. I had to know more." Just like Tim, Will observed. "Tim always wanted to know more, and he wanted to experience everything, and he wanted to know everything and everybody."

That quality had always been a part of Tim's make-up. He was a participator, not an observer. As a senior , he became fascinated with Ralph Waldo Emerson when he was assigned to write an English paper on the poet and transcendentalist philosopher, who emphasized spiritual individualism. Tim especially agreed with Emerson that studying life was not enough to understand it. A true scholar had to live life and experience everything possible.

His quest for experience led him to want to be with people who were different from him. His high-school girlfriend Heather Hancock knew him well, and summed up this aspect of his life in a comment to her parents when she and Tim began drifting apart. "Tim belongs to everybody," she told them.

As a result of his drive to experience all he could, his friend Katie Zurface said, "Tim lived in fast forward with a curiosity few could keep up with. He was confident, passionate, and he possessed a little kid's continuous yearning to see more of the world. And he had a great smile."

Tim was a big kid at heart, which in turn made him great at working with children, as reflected in a letter we received from another friend, Hari Ponnapula. The two had volunteered at a benefit event for a children's hospital. "Man did Tim love kids! I remember the time when we volunteered at Enchanted Forest. You played Santa, Mr. Kerlee! I was working the bubble machine, and Tim was pushing little kids on the train. He was so in tune and dedicated to what he was doing, that he was pushing the kids off the tracks! Then I would hear kids squealing with joy. At seeing the excitement, kids from my station would go to his station! Tim taught me to add enthusiasm to my work, so it's fun for me and everyone else."

Other speakers at the memorial service discussed the meaning of friendship and what a gift a true friend is. "So when you ask God for a gift, be thankful if He sends, not diamonds, pearls or riches, but the love of real, true friends," said Melissa Tate. Katie added that Tim would live on in his friends: "As long as one of us remembers our friend Tim, he has never truly died."

I will always remember Tim being described as the twelfth man of the bonfire collapse, and know that he and the other victims shall forever be linked with that Aggie tradition. He and they will live on as long as Aggies remember them. Knowing Aggies, that will be forever. Our pastor, Rick, briefly explained the significance of the Twelfth Man, after which Mid-South Aggie Club member Jim Clarke recited "The Last Corps Trip." Kelly Siebert, a friend of Tim's from Texas A&M, then lit the candle beside Tim's photo on the altar, and we sang a chorus of "Because He Lives."

> Because He lives, I can face tomorrow.
> Because he lives, all fear is gone.
> Because I know he holds the future,

And life is worth the living just because He lives.

After that uplifting song, it was my turn to speak about my son. I testified as to how God had answered our prayers. I wanted everyone to know that, although the answer had not been the one I sought, I knew that He had watched over Tim by keeping him alive long enough for us to say goodbye. I told them how we'd sensed His overwhelming presence in the hospital room and the peace it brought in the midst of our grief, knowing that Tim had been called home.

The church choir followed me with a wonderful rendition of "Majesty and Glory of Thy Name."

Keeping with the theme we had chosen for the memorial service, "I Have Kept the Faith" Rick opened with a reading of Second Timothy 4:7: "I have fought the good fight, I have finished the race, I have kept the faith." He then introduced his sermon by quoting from a scene in one of Tim's favorite movies, "Dead Poets Society," in which Robin Williams, playing a schoolmaster, takes his students into a picture gallery of those who had come before them.

He speaks to them softly:

"Now, look at them. They're not that different from you, are they? Same haircuts. Full of hormones, just like you. Invincible, just like you feel. The world is their oyster. They believed they were destined for great things, just like many of you. Their eyes are full of hope, just like you. And now they're gone. Did they wait until it was too late to make from their lives even one iota of what they were capable? And if you listen real close, you can hear them whisper their legacy to you. Go on; lean in. Listen, your hear it? Hear it? Carpe…carpe diem. Seize the day boys, make your lives extraordinary."

"Tim took that idea to heart," Rick continued. And for seventeen years he lived an extraordinary life; living life to the fullest, getting the most out of each day. We remember his infectious grin, how much fun he was to be around, his talent, his intellect. But these things, as significant as they were, were not the measure of Tim's life. Tim's life has a message for us. And what better way to remember Tim and celebrate his life than by asking what would Tim want to say to us.

"What would he say if he were here? First, 'Do your best!' You heard the words earlier from the scouts: 'On my honor, I will do my best...' For Tim, it was a matter of honor. Those words, 'I will do my best,' had an impact on all he did...If Tim did anything, he did his best. And he had fun doing it...Then he would say, 'Live life to the fullest and cherish every moment.' Tim loved life and looked for joy in everything. He could put his all into the most difficult question, the most complex math problem or most baffling equation—and make it look simple. Or he could let go, be silly, have fun and be himself, no matter where he was.

"Third, Tim would say, 'Be yourself.' Tim was unique...Some people said that Tim was his own person. But I think Tim was more than his own person—he was God's person. He knew who he was, but he also knew whose he was. And whether it was eating seaweed while everyone else ate fries, swing dancing when nobody knew what that was, or standing up for the outcast, he wasn't afraid to go against the crowd. He didn't bow to peer pressure, to what everybody else thought was the thing to do. And people respected that.

"Then, Tim would say, 'Don't live just for yourself.' Do something with what you've been given to make the world better. Tim found ways to serve, to make a difference. Even before Tim was an Aggie, he had Aggie Spirit, the spirit of the Twelfth Man. He was willing to step up and offer himself to make the difference.

"Then this: 'Accept and love all people.' Tim did that. About the only thing he would not tolerate in people was intolerance. He saw people for who they were, the content of their character, not the color of their skin or any of the other distinctions that divide us and cause us to build walls.

"Tim would say, 'Trust in God.' At A&M, Tim got a new nickname: 'David—a man after God's own heart.' Tim was playing the part of Israel's King David in a drama at A&M. But while that was only a part in a play, in real life, Tim was a man after God's own heart. Oh, Tim had questions and doubts, but he never stopped seeking answers. He got around and stayed around those who had faith and he talked with them, asked his questions, and he prayed. He kept seeking. Just like he lived life, he sought God.

"Then Tim would say, 'The Best is yet to be.' You see, Tim is aware of something that the rest of us can only dream about or read about. He knows the best is yet to be. For God has taken Tim's brokenness and made him whole; taken his death and given him life; taken his tears and wiped them away. And today Tim is alive—more alive than any of us. He is alive with God—alive to God. He's ready to serve, ready to take new risks, to continue the adventure. And Tim would want you to know that the best is yet to be.

"Finally, Tim would say this: 'Just as my life had purpose, my death will have meaning through you.' Whatever we remember about Tim is God's invitation to us to drink deeply of life; savor the gift of life; to seize the days we are given and grow closer to God. There is no grander sight in all the world than that of a person fired with a great purpose, dominated by the love of Christ. That was Tim. He left us that legacy. Seize the day! Make your life extraordinary!"

After Rick's sermon, Sherry Thompson, a church member and friend, sang "I'll Walk with God." This song has been a favorite of mine for years, but on that day some of those words were particularly meaningful: "There is no death, though eyes grow dim. There is no fear when I'm near to him." I had no fear for where my son was. I was sure he was in the arms of Jesus…or maybe whitewater rafting in Africa, or doing the Charleston with his grandmother, or right there with us. But wherever he was, he was in good hands—God's hands.

Chapter 6

Successful Living

"Train a child in the way he should go,
and when he is old he will not turn from it."
Proverbs 22:6 (*NIV*)

A reception in the church's Life Enrichment Center (gymnasium) followed the memorial service, giving my husband and me a chance to speak with many people we'd not been able to see in the week since Tim's death and to let them express their condolences. We greeted people for about two hours, and also watched Steven's memorial video on a large screen TV. The turnout for Tim's service amazed even those who'd traveled great distances to be there themselves. "I have never seen so many people at a funeral in my life, said Marion Scruggs, a cousin of mine from Virginia. "This is unbelievable."

I tried explaining to Marion that Tim's involvement with so many different organizations had helped him make friendships all across the city and state. Of course, that didn't answer the question of why he was so beloved to others—especially older adults and smaller children—who were not involved in these activities. What made him so special?

Many people have credited his Dad and me, and although I would like to believe that we "sculpted" Tim's great personality, the truth is we had been given great clay with which to work. Unlike many children, he listened to the advice offered by the adults in his life, including his father and me, teachers, and church and scout leaders. Tim, Sr. and I had done our best to raise him with proper values, but so do many other parents whose children don't turn out nearly as well as Tim had. So we credit him for absorbing those values and—more importantly—living them each day.

On the whole, I believe my husband and I managed to do a lot of things right, but we know we also made many mistakes. How often have parents wished that their children had come with instruction books? I know there were times when we did, but a presentation to our Sunday School class a few years ago by some teenagers in our church taught me that our children don't. This group of bright youngsters said they would much prefer that parents use their own instincts when dealing with their children's problems, and not rely on books. Ah, the wisdom of youth! Is it really only when we are older that we realize how much we can learn from others?

Parents always second-guess themselves. We all know of families in which the several children turn out completely different from one another, despite receiving essentially the same upbringing. In the debate of "nature versus nurture," I'd have to side with nature. It seems to me that people are born with a basic personality, and good parenting serves mainly to influence how it develops. And so it was that Tim, Sr. and I tried to influence our son to fully develop the wonderful personality he was born with. I suppose the fact that he was an only child made it easier for us.

For although Tim, Jr. had a half-brother and half-sister, he usually only saw them when we vacationed in Virginia to visit relatives. Once Sean came and stayed with us for a brief vacation, and Michele lived with us and went to college for seven months, but other than that, Tim, Jr. pretty much had our full attention. This enabled us to devote considerable time and energy to him, although I worried frequently if he was missing out on anything by not having brothers and sisters at home. With my husband paying child support to his ex-wife for Sean and Michele, however, we agreed to have only one child largely for economic reasons.

We were living in the Philippines when I became pregnant with Tim, Jr., my second pregnancy during our two-year stay there. We'd lost our first child, a little girl, eighteen weeks into the pregnancy. The miscarriage deeply hurt Tim, Sr., who had agreed to give his first wife custody of his beloved Michele and Sean, and he later made me promise that if he and I should ever divorce, that I would grant him custody of our child. Although he'd given up his daughter and elder son because he believed that children belong with their mother, he also knew he could not bear the pain of parting with a child again.

I knew that I would never leave him, so the promise was an easy one for me to make. Tim and I were right for each other, and we both believe firmly that the most important ingredient in properly raising child is a stable, secure marriage. Each of us had been married once before, when we were very young and unprepared for marriage. But by the time we found each other, we were mature enough to truly know what we wanted out of a relationship. I also think we understood what was necessary to put into a relationship in order for it to succeed. I thank God every day that we found each other.

We moved to Florida early in my pregnancy with Tim, Jr., and I did all I could to take good care of our unborn son and myself. I stopped working. I ate right, got lots of sleep, took my vitamins, and gave up all alcohol. I had never smoked, so that wasn't even an issue. Still, I worried that I would miscarry again, and wouldn't set up the nursery until the sixth month. I listened to lots of classical music and read books out loud. I don't know if these things really do stimulate children in the womb, but they certainly can't hurt. But I should have known, even before he was born, that Tim, Jr. would love to dance. During my pregnancy, we went to a pops concert at an amphitheater and that child was jumping and jiving to the music almost the entire time, until he finally tired himself out. I know he wore me out!

In spite of all my precautions during the pregnancy, our eight-pound, eleven- ounce son was born a week premature and jaundiced. We had the same blood type, so I knew that my negative blood type wasn't the problem. Although the doctor said that a baby his size shouldn't be jaundiced, he was. He spent his first week in the hospital, under ultraviolet lights. My husband and friends drove me to the hospital to breast-feed him and it was during one of these trips that a nurse told me, "That child is going to require a lot of loving. He cries and cries. I change him; I feed him, but as soon as I put him back in his crib, he starts screaming. All he wants is to be held."

Naïve new mother that I was, I just replied, "That's okay. I can't wait to just hold him and rock him for hours." Boy, was she right! I think Tim, Jr. and I spent most of his first three months at home in the rocking chair. The doctor had warned me not to let him cry for long periods of time and to pick him up if he didn't stop after a few minutes. The important thing was to make him feel secure and know that he was loved. Having been told by my mother that I was "spoiling him rotten," I tried letting him cry himself out a few times. I gave up after about forty-five minutes of non-stop screaming. It may have been inconvenient, but I know Tim never had problems with security and feeling loved.

I read to him, surrounded him with educational toys, and spoke to him in "baby talk" in spite of advice to the contrary. Years later, I have learned that many experts now believe the soft, cooing tones better get a child's attention than a normal conversational voice. We did everything we could think of to stimulate him, yet were still surprised at something he did at the age of seven months. He'd pulled the cushion off a rattan ottoman and began dropping toys between the wooden dowels atop the footstool, then started reaching underneath to retrieve them. Unable to reach one toy, he crawled to the kitchen and took a plastic spatula from a bottom cabinet drawer, then tried using it to reach the toy. He wasn't well enough coordinated to make it work, but he knew what he wanted to do. We watched in amazement, knowing that we had one smart kid! From then on, we had to work overtime to keep ahead of him.

We sang to him and danced with him to music, and we read to him. We read a lot, an experience that helped lead me to my current conviction that children are much smarter than we give them credit for. He genuinely seemed to soak in a great deal of what he was read. Once, when he was about eighteen months old, he bit the inside of his mouth while eating. As he cried, he began to utter, "Tigger…bee…Tigger…bee." I was flabbergasted! I'd recently read him a Winnie-the-Pooh story in which Tigger eats a flower with a bee in it, and gets stung inside his mouth. I'd had no idea that Timmy could have understood the story until that moment.

About a year later, we were visiting my mother in Hampton, Virginia, and took Timmy to a park and petting zoo. Here, he got his first experience with the sights, sounds and smells of a farm. Previously, he'd only seen pictures while I read from one of his favorite books, "The Animals of Farmer Jones." As I read him the story of the hungry animals calling to be fed, I would ask him what each animal would say, and Timmy would respond with the appropriate sound. Naturally, he wanted that story read that night when we returned to my mother's house, and I was more than happy to comply. When we came to the part where "the sheep sniff around the barn," I asked him what the sheep say. Expecting the usual, "baa baa," I was shocked when he wrinkled his nose and replied, "Pwew!" Obviously he'd absorbed more than I'd realized in his visit to the farm. In the future, I would be very careful about what I read to him, which television shows I watched when he was around, and—especially—the topics of conversations in his presence. He didn't miss a thing.

While I was the reader in the family, his dad's specialty was making up stories. Timothy's favorites were those in which he was the main character, usually the hero. So Tim, Sr. became the bedtime storyteller. My husband was always very generous with his time for Timmy, and infinitely patient and understanding. I doubt many fathers with sons would have been as understanding as he was when, at age two, Timmy said he wanted a doll.

At the time a woman who also tended several young girls was caring for him during the day and because they had dolls, he wanted one too. I thought it was a great idea—that it would help him grow up to be a loving father. His own loving father agreed, and he got his doll for Christmas. A year later, when the little girls from his preschool began ballet lessons, Timmy also insisted on dance classes. He turned out to be the star pupil, the one who stood front and center for the other students to watch in case they forgot a step. Reasoning that since more women enjoy dancing than men do, I figured our son would someday have his choice of partners if he could dance. How right I was. When he started swing dancing as a teenager, girls literally stood in line to wait their turn on the dance floor with him.

At home, the teacher in me wouldn't allow an opportunity for him to learn something slip by. By age two, he was counting the items on the table during breakfast. As I drove him to preschool, we would play "I spy" as a way of teaching him colors and shapes. For example, I would say, "I spy a green rectangle" and Tim would point to a highway sign. Or we would play "opposites"—I would say "day" and he would reply "night," and so forth.

He showed an early gift for mathematics, which especially pleased me as a math teacher. During a standard dinnertime negotiation over his vegetables when he was three, I told him to eat half his peas. He responded by asking what "half" meant. I explained the concept, and he ate them with no further argument. He surprised me the next day by coming to me and saying, "Mommy, I divided my book exactly in half. There are six pages on this side and six pages on the other side. Do you want to see how I did it?"

He proceeded to show me how he had placed down one page from the back and then one page from the front until he got to the middle of the book. Impressed, but sensing a chance to take the lesson a step further, I followed up my praise with a challenge for him to find half of ten. "That's easy," he quipped, holding out both hands. "Half of ten is five." Within a week, he asked how to find half of an odd number. He grasped my explanation immediately. Fractions would never be a problem for him!

Even higher math concepts—for a preschooler—posed little challenge for him. The summer he was four, he overheard me speaking on the phone about a summer program that we wanted him to attend, but weren't sure we could afford. I was between jobs at the time and a bit short on extra cash. "It's twelve dollars a week for four weeks. I don't know if I can afford that right now; let me get back with you," I said before hanging up. Timmy turned to me and said, "That's only forty-eight dollars. You can afford that." Puzzled, I asked him how he'd figured that out. "Well, four tens are forty, and four twos are eight, so that's forty-eight," he said. He was using the distributive property of mathematics and his ability to count by twos and tens to solve this problem! I was impressed.

At five, he asked if there were numbers lower than zero. I said yes and showed him a number line, then how to add and subtract using it. After a couple of weeks using the number line, he'd figured out the rules for adding and subtracting signed numbers without it. I remember how hard I'd struggled with the concept as a seventh-grader. My son was in kindergarten! Two years later, he was learning algebra. I'd ordered a "Hands On" equation kit to use with my seventh-graders. Tim came in while I practiced using the kit at home and said, "Teach me to play." So I did. And he did. The next day he asked to be shown how to solve the problems, "without the toys." Within a few weeks, he was solving some rather complicated equations. What a joy for a math teacher mother!

I will always be proud of my child prodigy and his wonderful early achievements. Of course, he wasn't a perfect toddler. At times, in fact, he could be a holy terror! Timmy was the most strong-willed child imaginable.

He was constantly into everything and insisted on his own way. At times, he seemed to understand that he was doing wrong but even that didn't stop him. He would reach for something, slap his own hand and shout "No! No!" and then grab it anyway. We tried everything to correct and control him. We tried time outs, we scolded him and talked to him, we sent him to his room (big punishment that was; we may have well have banished him to a toy store) and took away TV privileges. Nothing worked. Finally, once we knew he was old enough to understand and was just being stubborn, we resorted to spankings. They got his attention.

It's become popular in recent years to equate spanking with abuse, and I can't emphasize the difference between corrective spankings and beatings. We always spanked him on his bottom and although the swats stung, we never bruised or otherwise injured him. Most importantly, we never laid a hand on him in anger and always reminded him after a punishment that we loved him. We would explain why he was being punished, and that he had to learn to obey for his own safety and well being. He learned the lesson rapidly and, after only a few spankings, the mere threat of one was usually sufficient persuasion.

Timothy had always been extremely active, walking by nine months and running and climbing by his first birthday. Shopping trips were always an adventure, with him running off to explore. Afraid he would be abducted, or he might run off or get hurt, and knowing that he could disappear in an instant, I reluctantly bought a child harness. I used it when we were going to be in crowds or if his dad wasn't along to help control him. It drew many disapproving looks, but it was certainly better than risk losing my child. The harness didn't seem to bother him much. In fact, one day during an airport layover when he was two, he dropped to all fours and began barking like a dog. Despite the dirty looks I got, I had to smile at his wonderful imagination. Life with Tim was never boring.

As high-spirited as he was, I feared that never giving him his own way would break his will and didn't want to risk that. So occasionally, we'd let him win. As he got older and could make better arguments for his position, we would listen to him and go along when we felt that we could. But he did learn that once our mind was made up, all the whining and begging in the world wouldn't change it. In fact, they might even be grounds for punishment on their own.

As a teacher, I've encountered many young people who'd never learned to accept "no" as an answer. I suppose they're able to wear their parents down by arguing to get whatever they want. I knew I did not want my child to be like that. We'd hear his side on a matter, but once our decision was made, that was the end of the discussion. My constant prayer during that stubborn phase was, "Please, God. Please let his strong will work to his advantage when he's a teenager. Please let him want to do his thing and not follow the crowd."

Years later, I saw my prayer had been heard and answered. After his death, people frequently told us that Tim's most admired trait was the fact that he was "his own person." As one of his Fish Camp counselors, Jonathan Thompson, wrote us in a letter, "The confidence that he showed astounded me. I remember thinking back to when I was a freshman at Fish Camp and comparing myself to Tim. With the great number of campers in each camp, it becomes quite easy to let yourself become another 'sheep in the flock,' so to speak, and I was quite content in doing so...Tim was the **exact** opposite, he was incredibly outgoing, and very participatory, and he behaved quite admirably. I say this because he was simply being himself, and nothing else, and that, from the beginning, earned him my respect. He never seemed obsessed about what others thought of him like a lot of the freshmen often found themselves doing. He was obviously very comfortable with himself and his actions showed this well." Thank you, Lord, for giving me a strong-willed child willing to do his own thing and not succumb to peer pressure.

Tim's strong will and almost intuitive sense of right and wrong also manifested themselves in his personal heroes. He was an avid reader from an early age and, although he loved all kinds of books, he particularly liked biographies of people who'd defended the rights of others. When he was seven, he wrote his first "book." Entitled, "My Heroes," it was a collection of brief biographies of Martin Luther King, Jr., Susan B. Anthony, and Abraham Lincoln. Around that same time, he awoke us early one Saturday morning, running down the hall to our bedroom and shouting "Mom, Dad, I have the best news! Nelson Mandela is going to be freed! Isn't that great?" How many children his age even had an idea who Nelson Mandela was?

It was obvious that, even at that tender age, our son was committed to justice and equality. He'd had his only "formal" lesson about prejudice from me when he was about three or four, after he came home from pre-school and announced, "I don't like brown people." I kept my composure and asked him why. He answered, "Well, Derrick is brown; and he smells bad, and he bites!" Fortunately, Tim's preschool teacher also was African-American. I asked him if he liked Miss Gwen and he nodded. "And Miss Gwen is brown," I continued. He nodded again. "So," I said, "what you are trying to say is that you don't like Derrick and that he happens to be brown." He thought about it for a moment, then said, "I guess you're right." Those were the only prejudiced words that I ever heard my son utter. Between his exceptional math skills, his love of animals and nature, and his sense of justice, I didn't know if I was raising a future engineer, a member of Greenpeace, or a civil-rights leader.

In spite of his intelligence, Tim was not a "nerd." He loved the out-of-doors and played all kinds of sports, most of them very well. But Tim's athletic accomplishments weren't necessarily because of natural talent, but heart. "Timmy always gives one hundred and ten percent," a youth soccer coach once told me. When he won a league award for the player who demonstrated outstanding dedication, attitude, sportsmanship and team spirit, I could not have been prouder than if he'd just quarterbacked his team to a Super Bowl victory and been named MVP. His dad and I always believed that sportsmanship and teamwork are the most important things about youth athletics, but that didn't keep us from beaming with pride when he caught six fly balls in one tee-ball game and turned an unassisted double play by chasing down a runner and tagging him out. I was doubly pleased because fly balls had always been his weakness, and he'd spent two hours earlier that day with me, practicing catching them. His hard work paid off.

I'd mentioned earlier that Tim was something of a hellion as a child, but by the time he turned four, I was hopeful that we would all survive his early childhood years. It seemed he only misbehaved for us. His Sunday School and preschool teachers all thought he was wonderful! Given a choice, I suppose I'd rather have it that way than the other way around. One thing he wouldn't tolerate, however, was someone messing around with "his" girl. I went to pick him up one day from preschool, and the teacher asked if there had been any recent changes at home. I told her that his half-sister, Michele, had come to live with us while she attended college. She said she'd noticed a change in his classroom behavior, which had come to a head that day when he punched another boy for dancing with his "girlfriend!" Tim may have felt that while he had no choice but to share his parents, but his girl was his alone.

As sharp as Tim was, he also was a skillful manipulator of his parents. He was watching cartoons when I broke the news to him that his hamster, "Little Critter," had died the night before. I expected tears, but his only response was to look at me and say, "Oh, poor Critter." That was it, or so I thought. Apparently, his little mind worked overtime during the remainder of the show, because as soon as it ended he began to shriek hysterically. "My Critter is dead! My poor Critter! I've got to call my Nanny! I've got to tell her Critter is dead!" We calmed him down and made the long-distance call for him to tell his grandmother that his hamster had died. After he hung up the phone, he turned to us. "I think I know how I could get over Critter," he said between sobs. "I think (sob, sob) if you bought me a dog (sob, sob), I could get over Critter." It took all we had for Tim, Sr. and I to keep from cracking up with laughter. Tim did get his dog—four years later!

As soon as Tim started second grade, we signed him up for Cub Scouts. His Dad had been a scouting volunteer for many years and couldn't wait for young Timothy to become a Cub Scout, so they could share in what the program had to offer. Scouting is very family oriented and so, of course, we all shared in the experience. "Big" Tim was either a member of the pack Committee, a Cubmaster or a Webelos Den Leader, while I was a Den Leader, Cubmaster, or a Den Leader coach. Parents aren't required to take leadership positions in scouting, but involvement is expected and many of the rank requirements involve family participation. In an age when families seem to have so much difficulty scheduling time together at home, scouting offers a great chance to build strong family bonds.

A major theme in Cub Scout Leader training is KISMIF, or "Keep it Simple, Make it Fun." Games and other activities help children and adults learn to have fun doing silly, simple things together—things that cause them to look back, years later, and laugh fondly. Cub Scouting also teaches young people the importance of having—and living—religious values, respecting our nation and government, and doing good deeds for others. Tim incorporated the Cub Scout motto, "Do your best," into everything he did for the rest of his life. I've often thought how wonderful the world would be if everyone did, and tried my best to reinforce it when working with my scouts. Often when I was a Cub Scout leader, a boy would bring me a project he had been working on and ask if it was any good. I would answer with a question: "Did you do your best?" Most of the time, this would motivate them to go back and work a little more and a little harder on whatever it was. Otherwise, I would answer, "If you have done your best, then you can be proud of it." Yes, "Do Your Best" is a good motto for all of us.

Along with scouting, church was always important in our lives. I believe it's especially important to take children to church. They say that a person's basic personality, morals, and values are formed by the time he is five. If he has not had God and the teachings of the Bible as a regular part of his life by then, his spiritual growth will be limited. Waiting until children are teenagers and faced with all kinds of temptation to begin their spiritual training is probably too late to be much help to them when they are faced with tough decisions. Teaching and living these values should be a preventative measure, not a prescription for a life gone astray, and it is difficult to effectively convey spiritual, ethical, and moral values without the religious training found in the organized church. I agree that people need not attend church to be spiritual, but I strongly believe that the fellowship, support and encouragement of other believers is necessary for establishing a meaningful personal relationship with the Lord. This relationship sets our moral compass. Mealtime and bedtime prayers are not enough, and I regret allowing our family's hectic schedule to interfere with our plan to establish daily devotionals. This made it even more important for us to attend church.

My husband and I had wandered away from organized religion early in our marriage, but we joined a church as soon as we moved to Florida after I became pregnant. I wanted my child to have the same grounding in faith that I had growing up. I've changed denominations from the one I was raised in, after re-evaluating my beliefs and finding one closer to my own understanding of scripture. But without that basic foundation, I doubt that I would have had the knowledge or desire to make that decision. I also knew that being raised in the church and having a personal faith to rely on would enhance my child's ability to cope with the pressures of life, and so Timothy grew up with religious training as a basic foundation of his life.

We didn't just go to church on Sundays, either. We became active members, attending Sunday School and taking other classes, helping with Bible School, participating in service projects, and serving on various committees. For a time, I led the music during children's Sunday School, playing the piano and singing with more enthusiasm than talent. I managed to "make a joyful noise unto the Lord," and we had a good time singing the old-fashioned children's songs. Timothy especially loved them and threw himself into singing them.

Often, he would make up his own songs and sing them around the house. When he told me I should teach them to the other children in Sunday School, I asked him to write them down for me. Although they weren't of much value as music or poetry, I didn't want to discourage him. Besides, they were the heartfelt words of a loving child. As a result, I kept them for all these years and I'm glad I did for what they show of his beautiful spirit. "About Loving," demonstrates his lack of prejudice and love for all people, and its many references to different places also shows his budding knowledge and love of geography.

About Loving

I love you Lord
and I love everybody on this earth:
the Russian, the Asian,
the European, the Australians, the South Americans,
even the Eskimos up in the Arctic.
So every day I'm just a loving
up here in North America.

Another, "God is the Best," acknowledges God's blessings.

God is the Best

Now the Earth is bigger than an airplane,
and an airplane is bigger than a man,
and some things are bigger than others
        but God is the biggest of all.
Now God loves us everyday,
He gives us food for everyday,
He even gives us a Healthy and Happy life.
But what can we give him?
I know we give him love,
But what else can we give him?

How many seven year-olds would ask what could be given to God to show Him that He is loved? How many adults even ask that question? The Lord was obviously working in his life at a very early age.

Timothy enjoyed his Bible lessons and tried hard to understand them. Sometimes, of course, it wasn't easy for him, such as when he was four and mistakenly explained to me how Jesus had raised Lazarus from the dead by feeding him bread and fishes. When I told him that he had confused the stories, he became adamant and insisted I was wrong. I tried to explain that people can't eat when they're dead, but Tim had made up his mind, and so I abandoned the task as hopeless. At least I knew he had been listening in Sunday school to know that it had been Jesus who raised Lazarus, even if he'd gotten the method wrong.

In many ways, our otherwise exceptional son was a very typical boy— or at least seemed to be. Super heroes abounded in our home: Ninja Turtles, Silverhawks, Thundercats, G.I. Joe, and of course, everyone's favorite, Superman! Often, Tim would bring me a towel and ask me to pin it around his shoulders so he could fly around the house as Superman. And, so, the day I saw him walking around outside with an air of serenity and a dark blue beach towel draped over his shoulders, I asked him if he was being Superman. His look told me he thought I must have been stupid to not recognize him. He glared at me and in a disgusted tone said, "No!—I'm Jesus!" My first reaction was to hope that God has a sense of humor. But after thinking about it for a while, I reasoned that God would probably be pleased. After all, what more super hero and role model could a young boy have than Jesus?

I often tell people that Timothy's mind was like a sponge. It absorbed everything. Fortunately, this included the life lessons we taught him and he began to incorporate them into his personality and values. Our family life was almost ideal when he was between seven and ten. Life is never perfect, but those were certainly sweet years. We spent a year in Sicily during this time, and Timothy thrived. Fortunately, he had attended a Montessori School, and their view of education had a much broader scope than most traditional schools. He'd studied the Renaissance, and the teacher's enthusiasm for the subject had been contagious. Now Timothy was eagerly looking forward to seeing all the beautiful things and places he'd learned about.

In fact, when we told him we were moving to Italy, his first response was, "Now I can go to Florence and see the *David* in person!"

Many of the parents we knew would leave their children at home while they traveled and toured. Had we tried that, we knew we would have had a mutiny on our hands. The thought of leaving Tim behind when we went on our tours never occurred to us. There was also much to see right in Sicily. We visited the Norman city of Erice, the temples of Agrigento, the Greek ruins in Siracusa, Segesta and Selinunte, the Roman hunting lodge in Piazza Armerina, and the beaches of Cefalu. On one of these weekend tours, a woman approached me after the tour was over to say how impressed she had been with my son. She told me that she'd initially been disappointed to see a child on the tour because she feared the trip being ruined by some "spoiled brat." To the contrary, she now marveled at how good he'd been; she hardly knew he was there at all. He was there all right! He was just very busy soaking it all in and enthusiastically exploring the sights. I daresay he saw more than she did.

We spent three weeks touring the Italian mainland, and the highlight for Timothy was getting to see Michelangelo's *David* and the *Pieta*. He was disappointed, as many visitors now are, with the Sistine Chapel. Since it had been cleaned and restored, the once muted colors were very vibrant, to the point of being gaudy. He was also disillusioned with Venice, where he'd expected that gondolas were necessary to get around. He didn't know about all the bridges and walkways connecting the different parts of the city. Of course, we had to go for a gondola ride, even though the price was ridiculous. It just wouldn't have been Venice without it!

We spent Thanksgiving that year in London. I believe the traditional turkey was replaced with fish and chips, and we spent the evening at the theatre. In addition to four days in London, we also spent three days in Paris on that trip. It was nothing like any other Thanksgiving we'd spent as a family, but nonetheless one we'll never forget.

Tim was halfway through the fifth grade when we returned to the United States. The only problem he had adjusting, according to his teacher, was because he seemed too "worldly" for his classmates. Many simply couldn't understand the things he was talking about much of the time, but by the end of the year he fit in just fine.

I wish children could go right from fifth grade to high school. I don't know of anyone who enjoyed those middle school years. Those who say they did must have been the ones inflicting all the pain and suffering on the rest of us! It's difficult on a parent to raise a child to believe that violence is wrong and then send them to school where they are constantly kicked, hit, punched, teased and tormented. Once, when Tim came home from school to report having been punched in the stomach in the locker room, he added, "I almost threw up on him, Mom." I told him I wished he had. "That would have taught him a lesson." My husband and I went to speak with the assistant principal about it, and he pleased us with his handling of the situation. He called Tim and the two boys who tormented him worst into his office and told the three of them that he'd heard they had all been bullied. He told them he wouldn't tolerate and made them promise to come directly to him if there were any more incidents. "Don't even tell the teacher about it. Just tell them that I said you were to report to directly to me." Without accusing the two bullies of anything, he managed to put them on notice that future problems would not go unnoticed.

There were none; at least none for the rest of that school year. But a new middle school opened the following year in our district, and so Tim's problems began all over again with a new cast of bullies. We signed him up for karate lessons and, although he didn't learn enough to truly protect himself, it did bolster his self-confidence. We also gave him permission to defend himself, if necessary. The school's policy, however, called for disciplining both parties in a fight regardless of who started it. Once, when another student tried to hit Tim, he responded by holding him in a headlock until a teacher arrived. We thought Tim had handled the situation perfectly, but he was given detention for using "excessive force." I couldn't have cared less. He stood up for himself without hurting the other boy. Besides, once the word got around, there were a lot fewer problems with bullies.

Bullying and other middle-school problems took their toll on Tim, and his self-esteem began to falter. It was then that he found his salvation on the stage. Acting has always been a hobby of mine, so he'd developed an interest in theater at a very young age. When he was three, his father brought him to the dress rehearsal of "A Funny Thing Happened on the Way to the Forum." We weren't sure if he would make it through an actual performance, but it fascinated him and he sat quietly through the entire show. This amazed us. I had to stay behind for the director's notes and Tim threw a tantrum when I told him to go home with his father. "I want to stay and listen to the destructions!" he shouted. Since then, our family has referred to instructions as "destructions."

After watching me act in several plays over the next few years, Tim couldn't wait to try his hand at acting and when he was seven, we enrolled him in his first music, art and drama (MAD) camp through our church. Each year, the camp staged an original musical that set a familiar Bible story in modern times. Tim always landed major roles in these productions, and he continued acting in other school, church and community plays. For his role as Edmund in a local theatre's production of "The Lion, the Witch, and the Wardrobe," he was paid five dollars a performance with two performances a day. Most were during the week for schoolchildren. Including weekend shows, his first "professional" engagement totaled more than thirty performances.

Now in the eighth grade, his ego and self-esteem were getting a much-needed boost. The fan mail from young girls in the audience sure didn't hurt, either! The following year, he drew standing ovations as Gollum in "The Hobbit." He had found his special talent, while discovering that girls were just as attracted to actors as to athletes. In high school, his acting talent helped raise his grade in his least favorite class, English. He memorized and performed with a flair every extra credit monologue or speech the teacher assigned.

Tim had found something he was good at. He did it well and learned to use his gift to his advantage. But he also opted not to join the demanding high school drama group because that would have taken time away from other activities, and he had too many interests to limit himself to just one. But he continued to use his acting talent at church, where the ACTS group was a perfect fit for him. Whether dressing up as Cher or portraying Jesus, Tim put his all into the part. He'd found a way to combine his love of the Lord with his love of acting, and it didn't occupy all of his time.

Another saving grace for Tim during those middle school years was Boy Scouts. Besides the fun of camping and other outdoor activities, scouting also raised his self-esteem by awarding him merit badges and rank advancements. By the end of the eighth grade, he had earned the rank of Eagle Scout. In high school, he joined a High Adventure Explorer Post and went rock climbing, caving, canoeing, rappelling, and backpacking. These experiences built his sense of self-reliance and developed his self-confidence.

Scouting also taught him the importance of service to others. In addition to his troop's numerous service projects, scouting provided many opportunities to reach out to younger boys and help them through some of their difficulties. I remember one day when Tim looked out the window and saw the children next door, both Cub Scouts, playing with an American flag. He jumped up from the kitchen table and stormed out of the house, furious at the disrespect they were showing to the flag. He was gone quite a while, and when he came back inside, I questioned him on how he handled the situation. I was afraid that he had lost his temper with them, but I should have had more confidence in my son. He said he explained to them the proper way to treat the flag and taught them how to fold it correctly. He took a bad situation and turned it into a good lesson.

Another incident with a younger scout particularly stands out in my mind. Tim was on a "shake down" campout before leaving on a backpacking trip to Glacier National Park. A new scout and his father were along on this trip, even though they were not going to Glacier. Halfway up a mountainside on a hike, the younger scout said he couldn't go on. Tim told the boy and his father to stay there and rest. He was going on, but he would be back. Tim then double-timed to the top, dropped off his backpack, and went back down to the father and son he had left behind. He put on the child's backpack and led them up to the top. Tim had learned that by helping others, you feel better about yourself—one of the most important lessons of scouting.

The value of service that Tim learned at home and as a scout carried over into other areas of his life. I had told him once that his intelligence was God's gift to him, and that what he did with it was his gift to God. That became part of his personal philosophy of life and he used his mental skills to help others, tutoring his classmates in math, chemistry, physics, and even English. He also helped teachers and secretaries with computer problems. Once, an administrator called him out of class because of a computer problem that he needed fixed immediately! Many of his fellow students were better equipped than Tim was to handle some of the problems, and he managed to get them involved in service, also.

His willingness to help others and ability to motivate others to lend a hand were frequently mentioned by those who wrote down their favorite memory of him on index cards we passed out at the memorial. At least half of the writers mentioned his smile, his words of encouragement, his habit of "running you down to give you a hug," his friendly "hellos" and his willingness to help anyone however he could. Leanne Laub, a neighbor was having a hard time removing the Christmas lights that were wrapped around the trunk of a tree in her front yard. It was almost February and she was determined to get them down. Leanne recalled that "all was going well until the trunk divided into two higher limbs, and I realized I couldn't climb the tree (and I didn't want to) and unwind the lights." Along came Tim, who offered to help and was up the tree in a flash. He unwound the lights, then helped her wrap them up for storage. "Tim was always so giving and willing to help," she wrote.

Even on his summer vacation following high school, Tim was determined to help others if he could. Tim was the youngest member of the rafting party on the trip through the Grand Canyon we'd given him as a graduation present. He took it upon himself to help older passengers on and off the rafts, assist the crew with loading and unloading gear, or do whatever else needed to be done. He won the hearts of the rafters and the workers on the trip. We later received a letter from one of the couples on the trip, Fred and Carol Rogers. "Tim was everyone's favorite—we were his parents and grandparents for a week," they wrote. "He was truly an exceptional person and a great credit to his family. His enthusiasm for life, courtesy, helpfulness, intelligence, confidence, resourcefulness and so many other wonderful qualities endeared him to us." Their letter also mentioned the group of nudist senior citizens Tim had encountered on a hike he'd taken by himself, which he'd already told me about. "I tried to just look them in the eyes, but Mom, I saw more wrinkles than I ever cared to."

Other writers mentioned his passion for swing dancing. He loved to swing dance and to teach others how. Even if they stepped on his feet, a few his former students said, he would just laugh and not let them give up. Out dancing, he would pull shy ladies to the dance floor and not let them leave until they got the hang of it. He even taught his male friends (in the privacy of our home, of course) so they could dance with their dates. He also used his love of knowledge of swing dancing to reach out to the elderly. His Explorer Advisor, Mary Ellen Kemker, says that her favorite memory of Tim occurred after a fund raiser walk for Alzheimer's patients. At the completion of the walk, the participants had a reception with some of the patients. Big Band music was playing in the background, and Tim walked up to several elderly women and politely asked them to dance. Mary Ellen said the ladies glowed as they danced, probably reliving days long since passed.

Many also mentioned his contagious enthusiasm for life and fun, and his ability to get "high" without drugs or alcohol. Tim was strongly opposed to both. Once, in high school, he even turned in two classmates after intercepting a note they were passing that discussed buying acid for a rave party that coming weekend. School officials called both girls' parents in for a meeting, which at first infuriated the young women. Later, when he discussed the incident with me, he said he knew that one of them had never used drugs before and, "If anything had happened to her and I hadn't done something, I could never forgive myself. Her life is more important than her friendship." He didn't lose her friendship, either. She later thanked him for interfering. I was so proud of him for the courage he displayed!

His courage also led him to stand up for underdogs, becoming a champion for those who couldn't stand up for themselves. One such boy was a classmate in his freshman gym class who was picked on for being a little mentally slow and out of shape. Tim looked out for him, encouraged him and tried to get the other students to ease up on him. When that failed, he went to the teacher to let her know what was going on. Secretly, Tim found him just as irritating as did his other classmates. But instead of joining them in persecuting the boy or ignoring his torment, Tim took up for him because he remembered his own experience in middle school. He knew how it felt and did not want others to suffer the way he had. Tim had championed several young people in this way, and they were some who sang his praises the loudest at his memorial.

His near constant service to others and leadership ability earned Tim a selection to Bridge Builders, an organization recognized by former President Bush as a "Point of Light." Only two percent of his classmates were chosen to participate, which required multiple nominations from teachers as individuals with leadership potential and who genuinely cared about helping others. Its mission is "to develop among high school students, a group of future leaders who can lay aside individual social, economic, and cultural differences and work for the benefit of all." Of all Tim's many honors, I believe this one made me most proud.

Reflecting on his many fine qualities, I would have to say that the one that most stands out for me was his encouragement of others. Whether you were trying to learn to swing dance, solve a math problem or climb a mountain, Tim would be there to support you and make you feel as if you could do it if you worked hard enough. A fellow Texas A&M student, also a cadet, wrote to tell us that she'd been about ready to drop out of school and move back home because she was so upset about her parents' decision to divorce, until Tim talked her through her tears and made her feel better. He convinced her to stay, and she saw him the day before the accident. He gave her a hug and told her he was glad to see her still there. Tim realized that sometimes a listening ear, a hug, or a word of encouragement is all someone needs to overcome difficulties.

Another high school friend recalled a personality test that she, Tim and several other students had taken at a party. She said that the test revealed Tim to have a near perfect personality, while she was a bit flaky. After jokingly putting herself down several times about the test, Tim got serious with her. He told her that God had a purpose and plan for her and her personality, and that she shouldn't be putting herself down. That conversation seemed to have a real impact on her life because she began to view herself differently. She realized that God has a special plan for everyone.

Even Tim, Sr. and I benefited from his encouragement. Our climb together to the top of Angel Landing in Zion National Park will always be among my most precious memories of him. The climb is long and at times arduous. In places, we had to pull ourselves up the rock face on chains. The path narrows to only about six feet across at one point, with uneven rock and a thousand-foot drop on either side. Tim was incredibly patient with me. He encouraged me to stop often to rest and to drink plenty of water. When I wanted to stop and let him to go on without me, he refused. We were going to do this together, and I know that without his encouragement, I never would have made it. I would have missed that glorious view and the shared experience of conquering the mountain.

Tim didn't spend all of his time studying and helping others. He had to have time for girls! His senior year he dated Heather Hancock from October to May. Their first date was a Halloween party. Tim dressed up as a cheerleader and Heather as a football player. Their role reversal was the hit of the party. The next date, he showed up at her house in his 1940s swing dance suit. Fortunately, the Memphis area has a swing dance every two weeks for high school students. When he finally showed up at her house in regular clothes, her Mom commented, "You look pretty good in normal clothes, too, Tim!"

Their relationship made the senior year very special for both of them. The Christmas formal, Valentine Dance, and Senior Prom were highlights for Tim and Heather, but basketball games will stand out as my favorite memories. Heather was a basketball cheerleader, so naturally she was at every game. Since the high school colors were red and white, Tim would go to the games dressed in his red and white "Dr. Seuss" hat, his red "sixth man" shirt, and his red and white camouflage pants. He would stand in the student pep section and dance to the music and whoop and holler with the best of them. I think he was practicing to be an Aggie!

One of his first experiences with dating was with a girl named Angela, who was very involved in her church and frequently invited Tim to her youth group activities. When he asked her to functions at our church, however, she could never manage to make it. It seems Angela and her family were very devoted to their church and its beliefs, and they had more of an emotional approach to their faith than we did. We emphasized living the Christian life and demonstrating Christ's love through the daily living of our lives and our concern for others. The difference confused Tim, who began to question his faith and doubt whether we really were Christians after all. This led to several discussions about the different ways people express their faith. She had already decided to become a medical missionary and had vowed that she would not kiss a man or boy until her wedding day, and when Tim asked her if he could say that she was his girlfriend, she said she would have to pray about it. The next day she told Tim that although she wanted to say "yes," God had told her "no." At first, I didn't understand and doubted that God had spoken to her. I have since learned, however, that God can—and does—talk to us if we are tuned in to Him. Tim later joked about it with his friends, saying it wasn't too bad, being turned down by a deity.

Although things did not develop between Tim and Angela, I am grateful for their brief relationship for helping him shape his faith. After his death I read in his diary that she'd made him realize that his life had two parts. "I have my life, and I have my life with Christ," he wrote. "From now on, I am going to try to make the two parts become one." Within about two years, he had done just that. Everyone who knew him said that he lived his life full of the joy of Christ. He was one of the most upbeat people I have ever known. Oh sure, he had his bad moments; don't we all? But he was happy most of the time and wanted happiness for others.

That may have been in large part why so many people came to his memorial service. His was an uncommon form of popularity in today's age: He wasn't wealthy, didn't care about the latest fashions, drive a cool car, do drugs, smoke or drink alcohol, and never went along with the crowd unless he approved of what they were doing. He'd never accomplished anything the world would call monumental. But he was himself— no more, no less. Cary Hancock, Heather's dad, described him as "like some of those bigger than life movie characters that have a major impact in people's lives. Only it wasn't acting. He was a real person and through his life he did have an impact on everyone he met."

And he smiled. He encouraged people with words and hugs. He stood up for his convictions. He helped others and put their needs before his own. He lived a life full of the joy of the Lord and shared that joy with others. Because of these things, he was admired and loved by hundreds of people of all ages.

Chapter 7

There is No Death

"He who believes in me will live, even though he dies;
and whoever lives and believes in me will never die."
John 11:25 (*NIV*)

After the reception, we went back into the church sanctuary to retrieve the items that had been at the front of the church during the service. An assistant pastor, Brent David, had brought everything into his office for safekeeping. Also there was an oil painting of Tim. It was still wet and a note on it said not to move it for a few days, to allow it to finish drying. It really captured Tim's spirit! The dimples and gleam in his eyes shone with the brightness of his personality. We had no idea who the artist was because it was signed only, "Newport." Only later did we learn who had painted it and why.

The painting was by Colleen Newport Stevens, a well-known local artist and the mother of a young woman named Laura Gustaferro, whom Tim dated briefly in his junior year. We hadn't recognized the name because she signs her maiden name on her paintings. Laura and Tim had been on the German folk dancing team together. They'd also gone swing dancing a few times and she was Tim's date for the prom. They were only together for about a month because Tim wanted a more serious relationship than Laura did.

Colleen told us that the night Tim died, she awoke from a sound sleep and a heard a voice telling her to paint Tim. "Paint Tim? How can I paint Tim?" she wondered. Again, the voice told her to paint Tim. She immediately went downstairs to look for a picture of Tim, and found one of him and Laura from the prom.

She set up her watercolors, but the voice returned and told her to paint it in oil. "Oil? I've never painted in oil," she thought. She'd only taken one class in oil painting. But the voice persisted. "Yes, oil," she was told. She later reasoned that she'd been told to paint in oil because it lasts forever. Colleen set to work. As she painted, the voice guided her on exactly how to proceed. Tim was to wear a green tunic and be placed in a forest with two large trees surrounding him on either side. The sky was to be a yellow-gold color. Colleen finished the painting in a few days, and later said that she had never before experienced anything like that night. She said that it was as if Tim's hand was there, guiding hers. Upon seeing the painting, Jim Wheeler, commented that one of the trees—on the left side of the portrait—resembled an open hand.

Knowing how much Tim loved nature and the outdoors, I believe the picture captures what would have been his idea of heaven. Scripture tells us that there is no darkness in heaven, which would explain the golden sky.

This wasn't the only unusual story I was told concerning Tim. His high school girlfriend, Heather, said she'd had a dream about him the night bonfire collapsed and woke up thinking about him. When she heard the news of the bonfire accident that morning, she knew that he'd been hurt. In a later dream, Heather was being chased by someone who was trying to kill her. Tim found her and put his arms around her and said, "It's okay, Sweetie. You'll be all right. I won't let anything happen to you." She woke up immediately and, she insists, saw Tim standing over her, right before her face. "It was like a dream, but it wasn't a dream," she said. She has no doubt that she had a vision of him that night.

I have every reason to believe her. She's not the first person I know to have had a vision of someone who had passed on to the spiritual realm. I'll never forget a story my mother told me. One night she and my father were lying in bed, discussing my Dad's father, Sam Cross. Granddaddy was a very gentle, sweet man. After he retired, he took on a job as a crossing guard for the elementary school I attended. He died suddenly one morning while on the job. As my parents were reminiscing, my father suddenly asked my mother if she could see what he saw.

"Do you see Papa standing at the foot of the bed?" my mother answered.

"In his police uniform?" Dad asked.

"Yes, I do" she answered hesitantly.

I can't explain why some people see visions and other don't. I suppose for the same reason that some people are born natural musicians or intellectual geniuses and others of us aren't.

Many other friends of Tim had dreams about him. A neighborhood friend of my son's, Mark Laub, dreamed that Tim drove up in his driveway and got out of the car. Mark rushed outside when he saw Tim drive up and began fussing with Tim for scaring him so badly. He said that Tim started laughing and put his arm around him. Then Tim told him not to worry, that he was okay. Tim also put his arms around another friend in her dream, also telling her that she had no cause to worry.

Virginia Manner, a friend of Tim's who graduated a year before him, said she dreamed that she was going down a busy street when she saw Tim.

In her dream, she became frightened and ran away towards a park. Tim followed her and when she stopped to rest, stood a little distance away and apologized for frightening her. But, he told her that he just didn't want her to worry about him. Then he turned and left. Virginia said she was sorry for running from him; she would have liked to talk with him.

So, when my husband and I showed up at a scout meeting and a young scout named Roy walked up to me, put his hands on my shoulder and said, "I talked to your boy the other day," I wasn't surprised. In Roy's dream, he said, he'd walked into a Boy Scout meeting to find Tim sitting at a table. Roy sat down and they had a conversation. Once again, Tim stated that he was fine and everything was okay.

Others have said they felt his presence around them, although they've not had dreams or visions of Tim. A few days after his death, Debbie Ross, the mother of one of Tim's friends, said she woke up in the middle of the night and felt "a presence" in the room with her. "Tim," she said, "it's you, isn't it?" At that point, Debbie told us, she felt a tingling, like someone gently drumming, on the top of her head.

The mother of another one of Tim's friends, with whom she'd been having some difficulty, told us that as she sat in church around Christmastime contemplating her problems, she felt an invisible arm around her shoulder. A gentle voice told her not to worry—that everything would be all right. She believes that it was Tim sitting beside her, comforting her.

I have felt his presence on several occasions. The most vivid time was one night while lying on my side in bed. I felt as if Tim were "spooning" me, just as I had "spooned" him that morning in late October in the hotel room when we'd visited him in College Station.

Psychologists likely would dismiss these dreams and visions as coincidences, or explain them away as some action of the subconscious, yet each dream and vision had the same theme: Tim reassuring his friends that he was all right.

And God has always used dreams to communicate with people. The Bible is full of stories in which the Lord appears in dreams to give prophecies or make a promise. Why should modern times be any different? Perhaps it happens less frequently because we now have His word in written form, and by studying the Bible we can gain insight to His will if we let the Holy Spirit speak to us and lead us as we read.

But I still believe He speaks to us in our dreams. Why else would I have awakened in the middle of the night and had a specific thought to pray for Tim? Why would I have asked Jesus to wrap his loving arms around him and take his angels and protect Tim, especially while he worked on bonfire? I didn't even know Tim was working on bonfire that night.

It wasn't until that Christmas that I fully understood the reality of that answered prayer. My stepdaughter, Michele, asked me if I had seen the picture that had been in the papers and on the Internet showing Tim on the collapsed stack. I had heard about the picture from the day it first appeared in some of the newspapers, but had refused to look at it. A photographer for the university newspaper, *The Battalion*, had taken the picture, and I thought it insensitive and cruel to publish it. Michele said that she knew I hadn't wanted to see it, but told me that there were two angels in the picture. Of course, I had to see it then.

Michele printed a copy of the picture for her dad and me. Tim was lying there with a compound fracture of his right arm, his legs twisted in strange positions, and pinned beneath three large logs. He was propping up his head with his good arm and looking at the rescuer workers attempting to save one of his buddies. In spite of the pain he must have been in, there was no anguished look on his face. On the left-hand side, I saw an area of light above Tim and what appeared to be an angel with a surprised look on its face. But nothing was very clear until I saw it on the computer screen. There I saw a beautiful angel with long curly hair, and the surprised angel peeping out from behind her! Later, as I further examined the picture, I found another, childlike, angel sitting in the lap of the large, pretty angel. Other faces began to appear in both the light and dark areas of the photograph. There are at least six faces in that picture.

I have noticed that the resolution on some computers makes it easier to see than on others. Actually, the poorer the resolution, the better one can see the angels. The picture had been developed with a great deal of red in it, perhaps for sensationalism. But if it hadn't been for this developing, the angels might never have shown up. This picture has become a witness to many people about the existence of spiritual beings, and a number of them have responded to the picture on the Internet.

Some people never see the angels. Others see them only when they are pointed out to them, and some see them immediately. I told the teachers where I taught about the picture, and one of them returned to her room and brought the photograph up on the computer. As the students walked in they asked her what she was doing. The teacher told them about the angels and said she was looking for them. They became fascinated and started looking for them, too. One student went home and called up the picture on her computer. She called her father to come to her room, and before she could say anything, he exclaimed, "There are faces in that picture!" He obviously had no trouble seeing the heavenly beings.

The photographer was nominated for a Pulitzer Prize for the picture and although he didn't win, it did appear in "Life" magazine's "Year in Pictures." It was not published with the reddish tone, however, and only one angel can be seen—and then only if one looks very carefully. God definitely had His plan in mind when He had that photographer shoot the picture and develop it the way he did for the Internet.

Some may attribute the angels in the picture to an overactive imagination. But for me, it was just more confirmation that God did answer my prayer; that angels were with my son that night. How else could he have looked so peaceful and acted so coherently?

An event involving my stepson Sean's daughter simply cannot be explained as anything but further proof of angels. Four months after the accident, Sean's wife, Tracy, was putting the two and a half year old twins to sleep when Payton began pointing to the ceiling excitedly and yelled, "Look, look!"

"Look at what, Payton? The ceiling fan?" Tracy asked.

"No. It's a boy."

"You see a boy?"

"Yep!"

"Well, what does he look like? Does he have hands? Does he have feet?"

"Yes, he has hands. Yes, he has feet. He's all dressed in white and he's flying all around."

The next day, when Sean got home from working the night shift, Tracy told him about the incident. Sean pulled out a magazine that had pictures of the bonfire victims. "Do you see the boy that you saw on the ceiling last night?" he asked, while thumbing through the magazine. When he got to the fourth page, she said, "Yep!" and pointed directly to a picture of Tim, Jr.! Coincidence? Highly unlikely!

I should also note that Sean and Tracy keep only one small picture of Tim, Jr. on display in their home, and that the twins, Lincoln and Payton, had only seen their uncle twice in their lives—both times in their first nine months. And since they only attended church or Sunday School on special occasions, they weren't well acquainted with the concept of angels.

Carolyn Adams, the mother of bonfire victim Miranda Adams, has a similar story about her granddaughter, Tyler Michelle, who was thirteen months old when it occurred. As with Sean's twins, this also happened the March after the accident, while Carolyn and her husband Kenny were babysitting the child. Tyler was just awakening from a nap in her grandfather's arms, when her face suddenly lit up and she began to wave and say "Hi, Da-Da. Hi, Da-Da"—"Da-Da" being the family's pet name for Miranda used around Tyler.

She then babbled for a few minutes and then waved again and said, "Bye-Bye, Da-Da."

I believe Tim and Miranda decided to visit their nieces that spring. I daresay that those young children have some pretty good guardian angels looking out for them! What magnificent reassurance God was giving to us and to Tim's friends! We had a miraculous experience in the hospital room with Tim, feeling as if we were standing in the presence of Almighty God, but human nature lets doubt creep in. Was it in all in our imagination? Were we simply letting emotions rule our logical thought?

I believe that God gave these experiences to all of these people to let all of us know that we were not merely imagining a heavenly presence in that room. He is real; our encounter with Him was real; and the spirit does live on after physical death. I have no doubt.

Chapter 8

A New Life

"Speak, for your servant is listening."
I Samuel 3:10 (*NIV*)

Friends of ours from California, Paul and Clara Slaughter, stayed with us for a week with us after the memorial service. We'd known them since we lived in the Philippines, and they were wonderful in their support during this time. Clara helped me write thank-you notes and the four of us played cards together. That may sound weird, but the four of us had played spades at least once a week in the Philippines, and we always managed to work in a game or two every time we got together. We'd always played for fun, but now, concentrating on the cards kept our minds occupied so that we wouldn't spend every minute of that week dwelling on our loss. Just having them there helped us cope. It was nice to have good friends right there with us, giving us someone with whom we could talk, cry or just sit quietly.

That Tuesday, I went back to school to tell my students that I would not be returning until the next semester. I also wanted to give them a chance to talk about what had happened and to ask questions. The death of a young person, especially, affects everyone who knew them and their family. Many of my students had known Tim, but even those who didn't had seen his picture on my desk and had asked about him. They knew how proud I was of him and how much I loved him. I was close with many of my students and I felt a need to try to comfort them. A few asked questions that day, but mostly I hugged them and talked with them about issues on my heart. My message to them was simple: I told them the importance of not having unresolved issues with their loved ones.

"Fortunately, I had no unresolved issues with my son. If I had, I would have had time to resolve them and ask forgiveness before he died. There were eleven young people who didn't get the chance to tell their parents goodbye in this accident. Many people don't have that opportunity. Often our loved ones are snatched away unexpectedly. If my son had died and we had left each other with hostile words or bad feelings, then I would have felt guilty for the rest of my life. Don't leave the ones you love having had harsh words between you and them. Resolve your differences—you may never see them alive again," I said.

I reminded my students that teenagers and their parents often argue and have differences of opinion but even when they do, they should make sure that they know they still love each other. I challenged them to sit down that evening with anyone with whom they were having a problem and talk it over. "If they won't talk, then at least you will know that you have tried to mend the fences—and keep on trying; don't give up! Cherish each moment with your loved ones as if it were your last together," I said.

I also discussed faith, telling them that my husband I would never have survived the trauma of our son's death without our faith. Regardless of the religion they practiced, I encouraged my students to explore it deeply. Many people only call upon God in times of trouble; by then it may be too late. "If you are not used to hearing God and feeling his presence, it is very difficult in times of need to sense his peace and comfort," I said. "Practice your faith daily, so that it becomes a strong anchor and can hold you together when the storms of life strike your soul."

Most of them seemed to hang on my every word. I only wish they listened to my math lectures half as well as they paid attention that day. They would have all had A's! They were disappointed that I would not be back until second semester. But I explained to them that I needed time to grieve and be with family. My husband and I had been ministering to our son, his friends, our family and friends, and now I was ministering to them. It was time to concentrate on us.

Cards, e-mails and gifts continued streaming into the house. We received hundreds of cards from people we had never met. Most were from Aggies; some from people who had read our story in the paper. Many letters came from people who knew Tim personally and they related wonderful remembrances, but two letters from people who did not know Tim have left lasting memories. One was from Terri Anthony, who described herself as an elderly grandmother. She said she felt particularly moved to pray for Tim when she saw his name on the television screen, but expressed regret that her prayer didn't help. What she did not know is that Tim almost died three times on the operating table. Perhaps her prayer helped him to make it through that ordeal, in order for all of us to witness his beautiful, spiritual death.

The other letter was from a young graduate student who had joined one of the groups that visited Tim in the hospital. When I saw him at the hospital, he was wearing a shirt that said "Prayer Partner." He was ministering to the students in the hospital, both those who were physically injured and their friends who were emotionally damaged. Although he didn't know Tim personally, he said he laid his hand on Tim's foot and prayed for God to let Tim into His Kingdom. He said he received an immediate answer. "He's already mine." There was a time when I would have doubted the validity of his story, but now I have no doubts. I have seen and felt the awesome power of God, and I have heard him communicate to me.

The outpouring of love and concern was phenomenal. Many people made contributions to the scholarship that we established in Tim's memory, and a friend and local actor, Ron Jewell, performed a benefit performance of "Mark Twain" for that scholarship fund. Knowing our strong association with Boy Scouts, many contributed to the local Chickasaw Council, and because of many requests, that year's class of Eagle Scouts was named in Tim's memory. This proved to be very fitting because Tim had at least six friends who were in the 1999 Class of Eagles. Jay Sartain, who was the head of the Texas A&M Emergency Medical Service and who witnessed Tim's selfless acts and concern for others while he was trapped on the fallen stack, wrote a letter to the National Boy Scout Office, recommending Tim for the prestigious "Medal of Honor." (This was awarded posthumously in March of 2000.) We also received several books about grieving. I read a few, but didn't really have the time or energy to read them all. The ones I did read, however, were very helpful. We were invited to join a support group for parents who had lost children called "Compassionate Friends," and although it had helped many people, we didn't think it was right for us.

Friends visited and called, our pastor, Rick Kirchoff, counseled us. He said it takes three to five years to recover from the loss of a child, a piece of information that has proven valuable to me. More than a year after Tim's death as I write this, it's good to know that my tears and lingering grief aren't unusual. Recovery, of course, doesn't mean we ever completely get over it. Our life will never be the same, but the passing years will ease our pain. Rick offered long-term counseling, but we didn't feel we needed it because God was carrying us through. Our strong marital relationship, in which Tim, Sr. and I know we can discuss anything that bothers us, also has been and will continue to be a big help.

We received lots of practical advice during our counseling sessions with Rick, such as taking long walks together and seeing our doctor for a physical. Stress can play havoc with the body, so it made sense to ensure that any potential problems were taken care of early. But it was his spiritual advice that most helped us deal with our sorrow. Among other things, Rick told us to read our Bible every day. He said that devotional books were good, but that nothing could replace the word of God. We knew he was right and started reading the Bible daily. We also purchased a copy of *The Message.* Reading it made me fall in love with the Bible all over again. I hadn't been this excited about scripture since *The Living Bible* was published. At last there was a Bible written anyone could understand. Passages that had become routine and ordinary over the years, once again began to speak to me. I have gained new insight, and the Holy Spirit has filled my life and renewed my soul. My prayer life is stronger and I sometimes wonder how I had ever managed to get through my days without this support. Now, I find it hard to go to bed at night without having read some of God's Holy word. Daily reading and reflection on scripture has changed my life and sustained me throughout this crisis.

We had only been home about two weeks before we returned to Texas A&M for Silver Taps. Silver Taps is a wordless memorial service held on campus every month during the school year, if necessary, to honor students who have died during the previous month. I remember Tim, Jr. telling us how "awesome" it was, for so many people to come together at ten o'clock at night on the first Tuesday of each month to remember people that many did not even know. But they were Aggies, and therefore brothers and sisters. Attendance at Silver Taps is always high, but because of the bonfire accident December 1999's was an exceptionally large gathering.

Silver Taps is held in front of the statue of Lawrence Sullivan Ross, an early president of Texas A&M. On the night of Silver Taps, all lights in the area of the Academic Building are turned off and the bells of the nearby

Albritton Tower chime for fifteen minutes. The chimes cease precisely at ten o'clock, when the only sound to be heard is the rhythmic footfalls of the Corps' elite Ross Volunteers marching to their place before the statue. Because Silver Taps is a silent ceremony, I have been told, the Ross Volunteers keep step by the sound of their own breath. A twenty-one gun salute is fired, and "Taps" is then played three times by buglers atop the Academic Building. The buglers play one at a time, one each facing north, south and west. They do not face east, because the Aggies being honored will never again see the sun rise. The ceremony concluded, the Ross Volunteers exit by another sidewalk. As the sound of their footsteps fades in the distance, the assembly begins to dissolve in silence.

I had heard of Silver Taps even before our campus visit. But I remember crying when, during an explanation of the ceremony while we took our campus tour, we were told the part about not facing the east. Perhaps my reaction then foreshadowed what was to come for us.

The ceremony was beautiful and touching, and probably made more emotional than usual because of the bonfire collapse. Yet for me, it paled in comparison to what had occurred the night before at the same location. We'd arrived in College Station on Monday and saw notices of a prayer meeting to be held for John Comstock at ten that night. John had been severely injured in the accident. He'd already one leg amputated and undergone a half-dozen other operations in the attempt to save his life. Things were not looking good for John and many feared that another would be added to the death toll. But the student body remained convinced that twelve was A&M's number, and that John would pull through.

Naturally, we immediately decided to attend the prayer meeting. We arrived at the flagpole shortly before ten expecting there to be a small group gathered. Instead, there were hundreds in attendance. The crowd was so large we could not even get close enough to hear the scripture being read, or the prayers being offered aloud. The gathering was dismissed after about fifteen minutes but the students remained behind. They sat on sidewalks, knelt in the grass and stood in small groups of two to ten, and prayed continually. When we left about forty-five minutes later, most showed no sign of leaving anytime soon. We consider this experience another encounter with the living God. His spirit was there that night, and we were blessed to witness an event that I doubt would happen at any other public university. It was obvious to us that God was working on this campus. Finals were about to begin; yet hundreds of students remained gathered late into the night to pray for one of their fellows. Yes, Silver Taps was touching, but it was a ceremony. This was a powerful, spiritual—and spontaneous—event!

We were accompanied on the trip by my best friend, Rory Theuwees, and a young man from our church who was considering applying to Texas A&M, Patrick Boyd. Patrick had gone to the same high school as Tim and, although a year behind him in school, had been with him in German Folk Dancing and the math honor society, Mu Alpha Theta. They had also been in the youth choir and Methodist Youth Fellowship at our church. Rory came along to support us emotionally and in search of some closure for herself; she and her husband, Don, had been very close to Tim, Jr.

Although the word "closure" has become common today, I have come to despise it. I don't believe there is any such thing, nor should there be. I much prefer a phrase like "come to terms with his death." We can never close the doors of the past. People whom we loved and who have influenced our lives cannot be closed away in a closet, even when they are no longer with us physically. We wouldn't want to forget them or what they meant to us. Quite the opposite: We should want to remember them with thanksgiving and happy memories. Yes, we need to look to the future and not dwell on the past, which is perhaps what is meant by "closure." But I remain convinced that there is no such thing.

Also with us at Silver Taps were Laurinda, Beth, Melynda, and Margaret Appleton. Another person sat with us whom we'd never before met—Megan Kerlee Rooney, who had seen Tim, Jr.'s picture and name in the Bryan-College Station newspaper. Megan's middle name had been her grandmother's maiden name and the spelling was so unusual that she told her husband she knew there must be some relation. Although doubtful, her husband began searching genealogy sites on the Internet and discovered that she was, indeed, related to my husband. Megan's father had been Tim, Sr.'s first cousin. We knew that Tim, Sr.'s cousin, Larry Jones, taught at Texas A&M's vet school, but we did not know that he'd gotten married or had children. Most of the members of my father-in-law's side of the family had fallen out of touch with each other after leaving their home state of Montana. It was obvious to us that something had happened to cause a rift, but nobody knows what it was.

Megan told us that she never heard her grandmother speak of any brothers or sisters, and so assumed that her grandmother had been an only child. She became distraught to learn that she had had a cousin at Texas A&M, right there in her hometown, and had never known it until after he died. We met her and her husband, Bill, shortly before Silver Taps and asked them to join us. Megan came, while Bill stayed home to take care of their three boys. It was comforting, yet ironic, that at the same time we lost our son, we found some "long lost" cousins.

Patrick left campus that night knowing Texas A&M was the school for him. It would have been hard not to come to that conclusion after witnessing something as moving as Silver Taps. Rory left hoping her younger son would choose to attend A&M and join the Corps of Cadets.

Next, we had to face Christmas. After the death of a loved one, holidays and other significant dates such as birthdays and anniversaries, are always difficult times—especially the first time. Events that had always been eagerly anticipated become obstacles to overcome. We knew that the best way to overcome the difficulty of our first Christmas without Tim, Jr., would be to spend it in our home state of Virginia with my husband's children, the grandchildren, and other relatives. There is nothing like the presence of children to add to the joy of Christmas. Of course, this doesn't mean that we didn't have moments of tears and sorrow, but time with the grandchildren, nieces and nephews certainly helped ease the pain.

Michele's revelation about the angel in the photograph of Tim in the fallen stack also helped us make it through that first Christmas. Before she told us about it, I had been unable to look at the picture. But now, knowing that angels surrounded him, looking at it gives me comfort. Examining his face also reassures me. His expression shows no great pain, part of which, I'm sure, is because he was in shock—and I thank God for that body's defense mechanism. But although he was in shock, seeing the peaceful look on his face convinces me that God's angels were surrounding and comforting him in that time of great need. This is more evidence that my early morning prayer on that fateful November day was answered. Jesus did wrap His loving arms around him.

While in Virginia, I awaited some sign that the time had come for us to move back home to Virginia. I wanted that feeling because of my need to be near family, especially the grandchildren. It never came. The yearning that people often feel to return to their "roots" never occurred. When I shared these thoughts with my husband, he agreed. He didn't think we were supposed to move back to Virginia—at least not yet.

We returned to Tennessee a few days after Christmas. Tim, Sr. and I wanted to spend New Year's Eve alone together, but Rory insisted that we come to their house. She said they were having just a few friends over for a quiet evening. I guess things got out of hand, because their house was full of people. Tim and I wanted to leave, and I now wish we had: We were in no mood to party and feared we would spoil the evening for others. Somehow we made it through the evening, but it was definitely the hardest part of the holidays. At Christmas, we'd tried to remain focused on the true meaning of the holiday—the birth of Jesus Christ, Savior of the World. But the prospect of having a "Happy New Year" without my son, the light of my life, was impossible to contemplate. I could face one day at a time, but the thought of facing a year without him was overwhelming.

I managed to get through those first few months one day at a time. I would make it through a school day just fine after I returned to work, but the ringing of the bell at day's end would often find me bursting into tears.

I know I wasn't my usual self in the classroom. Before, I would make up songs and silly rhymes to help my students memorize things, and always put plenty of enthusiasm into my lessons. I know that aspect was lacking during that second semester, but I did all I could to hang on. At times, I felt as if I were in a trance throughout the day. Once again, I felt that God had put my life on autopilot, programming the computer and just allowing it to run. I began to focus more on myself, eliminating whatever extra work I could. I stopped grading homework and assigning projects. My husband and I needed quality time at home to heal.

No sooner than I had gotten back into the groove at school when another hurdle approached. Tim's eighteenth birthday would have been January thirteenth. Rory and Don offered to take us out for dinner that night to celebrate Tim's life. I declined, explaining to them that although they were the absolute best friends anyone could have, and that I knew they had our best interests at heart, we were not yet ready to celebrate. We would not rush our grieving. It is an important process and takes time. Instead of going out, we invited their family, along with Patrick Boyd and his family, over to eat dinner and to watch Tim's memorial video. We needed to be someplace where we could cry if we wanted, without worrying about being self-conscious about it.

Others remembered Tim's birthday by sending us cards, flowers, and e-mail—lots of e-mail! Michele had posted a notice about Tim's birthday on the Texags.com website, saying that we might appreciate some words of encouragement. The overwhelming outpouring of e-mailed support crashed our computer! We wanted to answer all the messages, but it took us days just to read them all. Replying to each one would have been impossible.

Once again the Aggie family had pulled through with support, and a few weeks after Tim's birthday, I shared with my husband an idea that has since changed our lives. We were driving down Germantown Parkway, and I remember not knowing how to address the subject other than head on. Uncertain how he would react, I hesitated at first. "You know Tim," I began, "I don't think we can have an experience like we did in that hospital room and just ignore it." He agreed, so I continued. "I think that we are supposed to do something for God. I'm not sure what it is. Maybe I could work with inner-city kids and help them with math, or work in a homeless shelter, or work with college students in some kind of ministry."

Tim replied that he thought himself best suited to work with college students, and added, "Maybe we are supposed to move to College Station and work with the students. There is so much healing that needs to take place."

My heart leapt for joy. That was exactly what I had been thinking, but Tim had always been the more practical, cautious one in our marriage while I was more impulsive. The chance was now before me to reverse those roles. I told him I supported his idea and suggested we think and pray about it before making a decision. But deep inside, I sensed some special meaning in the fact that we had arrived at the same conclusion independent of one another.

Discussing the idea later, we realized that as badly as we wanted others to share in our own personal encounter with God, doing so would be impossible. We could tell others what we felt and how our lives had changed, but we know that everyone must experience God for himself. Coming to know God is a faith journey and an adventure that is unique to each individual. But what we could do was teach young people and encourage them in developing their own relationships with Jesus Christ, in order that they might have similar experiences.

I wish I could say that God revealed His will for us through some monumental event, but that was not how He worked in our case. Instead, He spoke to us as we listened to sermons, as we prayed and as we read His word in the Bible. The only mysterious event was the arrival in our mailbox one day of a catalog of materials for working with church youth. I still don't know why it was sent to me. Then Laurinda called and invited Tim to speak at A&M United Methodist Church's Easter service. She asked him to give a five-minute talk about hope at their "Easter at the Creek" service, held in an amphitheater for an audience that typically exceeds four thousand, who bring blankets and lawn chairs for the event. Tim interpreted her invitation as a sign from God that College Station was where we could best serve Him.

Laurinda later told me that church attendance normally drops off in the spring semester, but that this year it had not. Each Sunday found the sanctuary overflowing with college students. It was obvious to us that the bonfire tragedy had set many young people toward God in search of answers to their many questions. I shared with her our belief that God was calling us to come and minister to Texas A&M's students, but also said we knew that it was not a good idea to make major life changes within a year of experiencing a tragedy. She gently reminded me that although that was generally a good rule, we should not put time restraints on God. He doesn't work by a calendar. We became convinced that God wanted us to move to Texas and work with students at Texas A&M. By the end of March, we had put our Memphis home up for sale.

We left for College Station to attend the Easter Services at A&M Methodist knowing that I would resign my teaching job, and we would move during the summer. That was about the only certainty. We had no idea exactly what we would be doing, only where we would be doing it. The Easter trip proved to be a busy one because Texas Independence Day fell on Good Friday, so there was Aggie Muster to attend. And now we would have to go house hunting.

Muster is another long-standing Aggie tradition. The annual memorial gathering for Aggies who've died in the year since the previous muster began in 1883 and a permanent date of April twenty-first, Texas Independence Day, was established in 1803. Knowing Texas A&M's military origins, I found it rather chilling that the Silver Taps for the Bonfire victims had been held on Pearl Harbor Day. Now Muster would be held on Good Friday. Along with remembering and celebrating the lives of Aggies who've passed on, Muster also is a time to renew old friendships and forge new ones. Events on the day of Muster include an on campus barbecue with entertainment ranging from performances by vocal groups to country-western dancing. A special ceremony, Ring Remembrance, was also held for family members of fallen Aggies who'd not earned enough credits to receive their Aggie Rings.

At Ring Remembrance each family was presented with a plaque bearing a replica of the crest found on the Aggie Ring. It had been suggested that families of current students be given actual rings, a suggestion that was receiving renewed attention because ten of the twelve bonfire victims had been students without sufficient hours to receive their rings. But because Aggie Rings are so highly prized and valued, university officials felt it inappropriate to give them away if they've not been earned. And since Aggie Rings are meant to be worn with pride, giving them away to be placed in a drawer or on a shelf to collect dust would be a waste. Ring Remembrance, therefore, would be an appropriate compromise. Sponsored by the Association of Former Students, it was held for the first time that April but it has now been added to the roster of Aggie traditions and will be held each year.

The evening Muster is a solemn contrast to the frivolities of the day. In addition to the ceremony held on campus, hundreds of smaller Muster ceremonies are held throughout the world. It has been said that Muster is to be conducted anywhere two or more Aggies can meet. I've even heard of Aggies in remote areas holding Muster over the phone. It is the most highly regarded of all Aggie traditions, and there are accounts of Muster in foxholes during World War I. In World War II, Gen. George Moore, a 1908 graduate, led twenty-five Aggies in a Muster Ceremony on Corregidor Island in the Philippines shortly before it fell to the Japanese.

Of course, the world's largest Muster is the one held at Reed Arena on the Texas A&M campus. The Aggie Band and the Singing Cadets perform, and speeches are made. The most moving portion of the ceremony, though, is the "Roll Call for the Absent," at which the names of Aggies who've died are read aloud. A candle is lit, and a friend or family member answers, "here," to show that the person remains with them in their heart.

Muster ends much like Silver Taps: a march-in by the Ross Volunteers, a twenty-one gun salute, and the playing of "Taps" three times. It is an extremely moving and emotional event, with its spirit perhaps best expressed in a poem by Dr. John Ashton, a 1906 graduate. As the last three stanzas state:

> Before we part and go upon our way,
> We pause to honor those we knew so well;
> The old familiar faces we miss so much today
> Left cherished recollections that time cannot dispel.

> Softly call the Muster:
> Let comrade answer, "Here!"
> Their spirits hover 'round us
> As if to bring us cheer!

> Mark them "present" in our hearts.
> We'll meet some other day.
> There is no death, but life eterne
> For our old friends such as they!

Although Muster had left us emotionally exhausted, we knew that we had to use our time on Saturday to look for a house. We'd contacted a real estate agent before leaving Memphis, and we looked at seven or eight houses that day. Our original plan had been to simply let the agent know the type of house and location we desired, and ask him to stay "on the lookout" for something appropriate. However, we found one that we liked and took the greatest leap of faith in our lives by putting a contract on it. We'd not yet found a buyer for our home in Tennessee, but believing firmly that God wanted to use us in Texas, we signed on the bottom line that evening.

Easter was glorious! Although windy, it was a sunny, picture-perfect, spring morning. As I greeted people with, "He is risen!" and awaited the response, "He is risen, indeed!" the cross and Christ's resurrection took on a deeper and much more personal meaning for me. All of our immediate family had come to College Station for Muster and stayed for the Easter service. We had dinner at the home of Megan and Bill Rooney and although Tim and I had to leave after dinner because we had an earlier flight than the others, the twins, Lincoln and Payton, hunted Easter eggs with Megan and Bill's three children: Will, David, and Travis. It was good to celebrate Easter with family.

By the time we returned to Tennessee, we were both emotionally drained and physically exhausted. In spite of our fatigue, a lot had to be done. We slowly started packing two or three boxes a day and the garage began to fill up. We'd planned to close on the house in College Station at the end of May, and move out of our house in Bartlett in the middle of June. This would leave us time to go to Texas for the closing, head west to spread Tim's ashes and pack a few last things before the relocation.

About a week after finalizing all of these details, we received an offer on our house. The buyers told us that their desired move-in day was the same day we'd planned to move out, but agreed to a one-day delay when told we couldn't change our moving date. Coincidence? Believe that if you wish, but for me, it was the work of God. We had learned yet another valuable lesson about faith. Faith is not a belief in something you cannot see or prove; it is obedience without reservation. To get faith, you have to practice it. As the old saying goes, "Actions speak louder than words."

As soon as school ended for me, we traveled to College Station to close on our new home, then left immediately for New Mexico to spread Tim's ashes at the Boy Scout National Reservation, Philmont. It turned out to be a beautiful ceremony in the New Mexico mountains, the experience made all the more special by the presence of ten of Tim's friends from Texas A&M and a university staff member, Lt.Col. Mike Caudle. The time together gave us an opportunity to get to know some of the students at a deeper level, for which I will always be grateful. It felt so good to laugh and cry together with them as we remembered my son. I'm also grateful to a Memphis physician named John McCall, who had read in the paper about Tim's death and our plans for his ashes and offered us the use of his cabin in the area for a few days.

We were unable to spread Tim's ashes exactly where he'd requested because we did not want to violate the traditions and beliefs of the Native Americans in the area. We did, however, find an equally beautiful spot in an appropriate location. Tim's Explorer leader, Mary Ellen Kemker, flew in from Memphis to lead the ceremony. Tim and I stayed behind for two days after everyone else left, for a badly needed retreat from the world. We'd planned to stay a third day, but I guess we had all the seclusion that we could handle and returned to Bartlett.

The most difficult part of the transition to our new life was leaving our church family and our many friends in Tennessee. There were some tearful goodbyes, but we never doubted we were doing the right thing. We have moved many times and always because we wanted the change, but each move had been marked by a sense of trepidation. Not so in this case. We had no doubts or misgivings about our decision—and what a major decision it was! This was no mere change of address we faced— it was a complete change of purpose and of our life's mission. Instead of teaching math and being the mother of one child, I would now seek to influence college students and help them with something much more meaningful and important than mathematics. We would try to lead and guide these young people's spiritual development while being supportive friends and confidantes in life's difficult moments. "If we thought about it, we would probably be scared," I had told a Memphis reporter before leaving. Our income would be cut in half, and we didn't know exactly how we would carry out our mission. Regardless of the major lifestyle changes and additional responsibilities, we were eagerly looking forward to our new life.

We moved in our new home on June eighteenth. About two weeks later, we met with the new pastor at A&M United Methodist Church, Jerry Neff; the new assistant pastor in charge of College Ministries, Deborah Proctor; the head of the College Ministries Committee, Linda

Brochu; and Laurinda Kwiatkowski, director of Youth Ministries. When they asked us what we planned to do there, my honest answer was "We don't know." I did know that our goal was to help students develop personal relationships with Jesus Christ. We didn't care if they were Methodist, Baptist, Catholic or Episcopalian. Their backgrounds were unimportant to us, and we would not try to convert them to Methodism.

"We just want to help them heal from the Bonfire tragedy and be spiritually prepared for the next blow that life may deal them," I said. "It seems that this church is doing a good job of ministering to the students who attend here and who are seeking God. Our goal is to reach students who may not be attending church or a Bible study regularly, and help them grow in their faith."

Although we didn't have a plan in place when we arrived, doors began opening almost immediately. Besides attending training sessions at the church on leading small groups, we also attended training at a church in nearby Temple, on how to use "Serendipity" material. One thing I like about the "Serendipity" program is that one need not be an expert on the Bible to lead groups. Questions are open-ended and encourage participants to share their faith in small group settings. It also involves examining small portions of scripture and then answering questions designed to help apply scripture to daily life. In this way, the Bible becomes more than a history book; it becomes a guidebook for life. We completed the training and bought some "Serendipity" materials, confident in our ability to lead a group.

The Lord opened another door for us when members of our son's Corps squadron asked us to lead a Bible study for upperclassmen. The group has grown rapidly and we are pleased with the great spiritual growth of its faithful members. We also started a second Sunday School class at the church for college age adults. Tim and I had taken a class in spiritual discipline at our church back home, and we now attend a Disciple Bible study at A&M Methodist, as well as a study of the book of Luke. These keep us spiritually fed and give the additional knowledge to do a better job with the Bible studies we lead.

We joined and became active members of the College Ministries Board. Working with this committee, we have helped organize a barn dance and a Christian concert, staffed a retreat, helped compile finals "survival kits" for students, cooked "welcome back" meals and helped with freshmen move-in day. Among my favorite duties is serving on the church's "Howdy Patrol." "Howdy" is the official greeting at Texas A&M, and so members of the patrol greet young people arriving at church with a handshake or a hug and, of course, a great big "Howdy!"

We have also established "Fish Fridays," a weekly gathering at our home for fish in the Corps or any other freshman at the university. We serve a light dinner and socialize. This gives them a chance to escape from Corps or dorm life for a while, enjoy a home-cooked meal and play games or watch a movie. Occasionally, students will spend the night. We've even had cadets spend a weekend when they've been ill. A dorm room is no place to be when a cadet is sick.

As word has gotten out about us being here and wanting to help young people, many students have come by our home for a meal and some comforting words. We are not professional counselors, nor do we profess to be. But we listen well and give great hugs. Students know that someone truly cares about them and is praying for them, and that they are always welcome in our home. Some weeks pass fairly calmly, while others are nonstop activity. Personally, we prefer them busy because that means we're helping more people.

Our first semester here was a particularly busy one. After the accident, the university commissioned an investigation by an independent Special Commission on the 1999 Bonfire. The commission's report was released in early May, revealing how little supervision the university had exercised over the building of the giant structure. Students who knew little or nothing about engineering had made design changes that greatly affected the integrity of the stack. Gradually, over years of subtle changes, little remained that resembled the original plan. In response to the commission's report, university President Ray M. Bowen ordered a two-year moratorium on Bonfire and recommended other changes when the tradition resumed. Among these were that future bonfires would be designed, and construction supervised, by engineers and other professionals. A group of students objecting to the decision launched a campaign for an off-campus bonfire and formed a group called, "Keep the Fire Burning."

The very idea badly frightened Tim and me. We wanted to spare any parent from ever going through what we'd just experienced. As much as bonfire meant to these students, no tradition was worth the risk of losing another human life. So we undertook a personal campaign of speaking to students at every opportunity available to discourage them from participating in an off-campus bonfire. We also were invited to several dorms and meetings of campus organizations to share our thoughts on the matter

We also served on a committee to plan the November remembrance ceremony, largely as liaisons between other parents of bonfire victims and the committee. The week prior to the memorial was a hectic one, with us scheduled to speak at two different functions. "Rebuild" was an educational program about Bonfire for freshmen and new transfer students. We focused our presentation mainly on the wonderful support we received from the College Station community and the Aggie family in the aftermath of the bonfire accident. We'd noted that, after the accident, sorrow had many students hanging their heads and failing to give the traditional Aggie greeting of "Howdy." It had resumed somewhat that semester, but still remained less frequent than before the accident. We encouraged these freshmen to reinstate the tradition of "Howdy" and to hold their heads high: They had much to be proud of at Texas A&M.

Kyle Easley, the Corps' chaplain, had organized the second event. He asked us if we would address students in Rudder Theater in the week leading up to the remembrance. We spoke on "Finding God's Purpose in the Face of Tragedy" and tried to make two main points. First of all, that each of our lives is affected by disappointment, hardship, and tragedy and the best way to handle them is by being spiritually prepared. We told the young people that we prepare ourselves spiritually through prayer, reading and reflecting on scripture, and fellowship with other believers. Second, we told them that the truest test of our faith is in how we react to the tough times. We can turn inward and dwell in self-pity, or we can turn outward and try to help others. When we find a creative way to reach out to others, we inadvertently help ourselves. In our case, the love that we would have given our son, we now give to scores of other students. This enables us to heal and, hopefully, we are making a difference in the lives of others.

We opened the floor to questions, and I was momentarily thrown when a young woman asked me, "Are you happy?"

"I can tell you this," I told her after a brief pause to recover. "I know that I am living in the will of God, and there is no greater joy than knowing that you are in His will. Are you asking me if I grieve? Every day. I have moments of happiness, but happiness and joy are not the same thing. Happiness is fleeting. It doesn't last. Joy is much deeper and constant. I am full of the joy of the Lord because I know that I am doing exactly what He wants me to do."

I've found many students are fascinated with the subject of God's will, perhaps because they are still seeking what to do with their own lives. Consequently, we began leading a Bible study on the "Will of God." Before discussing God's will for the students' lives, we determined to first understand what is meant by the phrase. We found some great insights in Leslie Weatherhead's book, *The Will of God*. It also confirmed some of my own ideas, such as the belief that God wants only good things for His children. Weatherhead terms this His "intentional will." Because of man's free will and the laws of nature, however, bad things sometimes just happen. But God has the ability to make something good out of tragedy or suffering— if we let Him. What matters is how we react to bad circumstances. If we act in manner that brings glory to God, then His "circumstantial will"—what He wishes to happen in those circumstances—can be realized.

Weatherhead also sets forth a three-part test to determine if we are cooperating with God to bring good from evil. First, will my actions serve mankind in some way? Then, will my actions or attitudes satisfy a true need? Finally, are my actions or attitudes in harmony with both my personal and spiritual values? Acting in cooperation with God to carry out His circumstantial will opens the way for His ultimate will—for people to receive Christ as their savior in order to join him in heaven—to be done.

It was not God's intentional will for the bonfire to fall that night, killing and maiming all those beautiful children. But the sins of pride and arrogance led its builders to a false sense of infallibility. Over the years, they came to feel confident in making decisions on structural and design changes that they were not qualified to make. Well-meaning people unwittingly attempted to build a structure in defiance of the laws of nature, and gravity won. Except in the case of miracles, God does not intervene to stop catastrophes.

The question for those of us touched by this tragedy then becomes, "How do we react in a way to help God carry out His circumstantial will?" What good can come of such a catastrophe? How can God use this horrible accident to bring His children closer to Him and eventually welcome them into His arms in heaven? I have personally witnessed much good come about as a result of the accident. For one thing, many young people on campus started going to church, seeking out God for answers to their many questions. The increase in church attendance continues. Many people have written or told us that the bonfire tragedy caused them to consider their own mortality, and how important it is to develop a relationship with God.

On the first anniversary of the accident, I received a letter from one of Tim's high school friends, Lauren Hill. "I hope that it will give you comfort to know that I am a Christian today because of Tim," she wrote. A young woman he'd met at Fish Camp, Courtney Cox, approached me after one of our talks on campus and also credited him with helping renew her faith. "He was such an amazing person and so strong in his faith. I go to mass every Sunday now because of Tim. I feel a great comfort and sense of peace when I'm at church. I'll never forget him, and I want to have the kind of faith that he had."

Another correspondence I received shortly after Tim's death showed me that God can work through disasters to bring people closer to Him. It was from Stacey Lawler, who attended the Governor's School for the Sciences with Tim in the summer of 1998. Stacey collected and printed out all of the e-mail that she and the other students had exchanged after learning of Tim's death. It had been a life-changing experience for many.

As one young man wrote, "One of the main points I thought of is what would happen if it were me instead. Then it hit me: an amazing revelation that I will take with me and use to better myself for the rest of my life. I realized that very few people would care. I realized that throughout my life I have done nothing but alienate people (and myself in the process) by looking down on them and ridiculing them when I should be befriending them. I always thought that I was so great. From reading all of these e-mails about how great and wonderful Tim was (and he certainly was), I realized that I have no concept of what true greatness is. It's not the amount of knowledge, power, or wealth that one amasses throughout his life as I had thought previously. It's the people he affects during his stay here. I suppose I'll end this by saying that Tim was most certainly an amazing person if he can affect me and make me change my views even after his death. Also, being that I am atheist, I would like to tell you all that I hope with all of my heart and mind that there is a Heaven and that the gates are standing wide open for him when he gets there." Since reading his e-mail, I have prayed that this young man discovers that there truly is a Heaven and a loving God who rules over it. Perhaps Tim's death didn't bring this young man to God, but at least he's thinking and hoping about heaven. A seed has been planted.

The most obvious sign to us of God using this accident to touch the lives of others was a very personal one. This past Christmas, my husband and I witnessed the answer to a long-term prayer of ours. A week before

Christmas 2000, we attended the baptism of our son, Sean, and his wife, Tracy. We had prayed for years that they would accept Jesus Christ as their Lord and Savior. Sean had always said he didn't believe he was "good enough to be a Christian." He told this to the pastor of the Baptist church they began attending after the twins started its Bible School, and the pastor explained to him that none of us are "good enough"—that's why Jesus had to die for our sins. The Perfect One took unto himself the sins of all the world, paying with His life for our way to heaven. All we have to do is accept God's gracious gift. Sean and Tracy have chosen to accept salvation from the only hand that can give it. Thank God! The connection with Tim's death was reflected in a note in Sean's birthday card to Tim, Sr. that November. "I know that Tim's death has been hard on you," he wrote, "but it has brought us all closer to the Lord." Obviously, our son's death had caused Sean and Tracy to seek out God. His father and I are just grateful that there were other people in their lives to help them find their way.

Tim's life had always influenced the lives of my husband and myself, including drawing us back toward God and the church from which we had strayed. We knew that we wanted to raise a child with Christian values, and so began attending church while I was pregnant. As I attempted to teach him about God and faith, my own faith increased and I learned much from my child. Often, my lessons for Tim turned into self-instruction. Because I wanted him to be patient and tolerant, I sought to set an example by practicing patience and tolerance toward others. Or, I would notice behaviors or habits in him that I didn't like and wonder where he had learned them. Self-examination would then reveal that he had picked them up from me and would cause me to change my ways.

Just as Tim tried to bring others closer to the Lord in his life, his death brought his father and me closer to Him than we had ever been. As my husband told me a few months after Tim's death, "I believe. I've always believed. But it's a shame that my son had to die in order for me to get so close to the Lord." Yes, it is a shame. But it's also true for me. The loss of our son has been a very personal lesson to us that God can use tragedy for

His glory and our good. We have never before felt more at peace with our lives, or more confident in our values and purpose in this world. And there is absolutely no fear of death, because we know with all our hearts that we will be reunited with our son. I suppose we didn't say "goodbye" to Tim after all. We just said, "See you later, Buddy."

We now know that God is using us to help others develop a close, personal relationship with Christ. I've lost count of the people, young and old, who have approached us to say what a blessing and inspiration they received from my son's life and our reaction to his death. Perhaps the greatest compliment I've ever received came from Emily Porterfield, who'd been a fish with Tim in Squadron 16 and now attends our Bible study. "I used to think that being a Christian was a duty or obligation," she told me. "Through these Bible studies I have come to realize that it is a privilege to be a Christian." The compliment for me lies in the fact that God has used us to help at least one person realize the joy of being a Christian. If we have achieved this, then our work in College Station has not been in vain.

We are often asked about our long-term plans. In truth, I don't know what they are. I do know that God has led us to College Station and nothing else matters. He may direct us somewhere else in the future, or we may end our days here. It makes no difference to us where we are, because God will be there with us.

Appendix

Bonfire Relief Fund, Memorials, and Scholarships

All profits from the sale of this book will be donated either to the Tim Kerlee, Jr. Memorial Scholarship Fund, to the Bonfire Relief Fund, or to Campus Ministries at A&M United Methodist Church.

The **Bonfire Relief Fund** gives financial help to those accident survivors who continue to have medical expenses. I am happy to report that John Comstock is now able to walk with the use of a walker, and plans to return to Texas A&M in the fall of 2001 to continue his education. He has incurred over a million dollars of medical expenses and still faces surgeries, physical therapy, and a lifetime of related expenses. The Bonfire Relief Fund helps him and other accident victims with these expenses. If you feel led to donate to this fund, make your check out to "The Association of Former Students," and write "Bonfire Relief Fund" in the memo section of the check. Mail to:

Bonfire Relief Fund
The Association of Former Students
505 George Bush Drive
College Station, TX 77840-2918

The **Bonfire Memorial Fund** will support permanent recognition of those who died in the accident. Checks should be made out to "Texas A&M Foundation" with "Bonfire Memorial Fund" written in the memo section. Mail to:

Bonfire Memorial Fund
Texas A&M Foundation
401 George Bush Drive
College Station, TX 77840-2811

The **Miranda Adams Scholarship Fund** will be used to grant scholarships to Sante Fe High School graduates who are actively involved in many aspects of their school and community. Contributions should be mailed to:

Miranda Adams Scholarship Fund
Southwest Bank of Texas
PO Box 27459
Houston, TX 77227-7459

The **Christopher Breen Memorial Scholarship Fund** has been established by his family and friends to help provide financial support to a student in the South Texas Law School Advocacy program. Contributions should be mailed to:

The Christopher Breen Memorial Scholarship
South Texas College of Law
Houston, TX

Contributions can be made to the **Michael Ebanks Memorial Aerospace Scholarship** by noting "Michael Ebanks Memorial Aerospace Scholarship" in the memo section of the check and mailing it to:

Texas A&M Foundation
401 George Bush Drive
College Station, TX 77840-2811

Contributions made to the **Jeremy Frampton Memorial Fund** will be used to support Jeremy's House, a shelter for children and parental learning center. Mail checks to:

Jeremy Frampton Memorial Fund
Farmers and Merchants Bank
301 East Main
Turlock, CA 95382

The **Jamie Hand Memorial Scholarship Fund** will be used to help support graduating Henderson High School seniors going to Texas A&M University. Checks should be mailed to:

Jamie Hand Memorial Scholarship Fund
Citizen's National Bank
PO Box 1009
Henderson, TX 75653

The **Timothy Doran Kerlee, Jr. Memorial Scholarship** will financially assist out-of-state students who wish to be a member of the TAMU Corps of Cadets and major in engineering. Contributors should write "Tim Kerlee Scholarship" in the memo section of the check and send to:

Texas A&M Foundation
401 George Bush Drive
College Station, TX 77840-2811

To honor Lucas Kimmel, the Nueces County A&M Club created the **Lucas Kimmel Scholarship**. Donations to this fund can be made by sending a check to:

Lucas Kimmel Scholarship
Nueces County A&M Club
Corpus Christi, TX

A chapel will be built at the Sid Richardson Scout Reservation in Bridgeport to honor **Chad Powell**. Those wishing to help with this project may send contributions to:

Chad Powell Memorial Fund
Frost National Bank—Keller Branch
C/O Jay Sharp
PO Box 16509
Ft. Worth, TX 76162

About the Author

Janice Kerlee is a native of Hampton, Virginia and has her BS and MS in Mathematics Education from Old Dominion University in Norfolk, Virginia. She and her husband Tim invite you to E-mail them (tkerlee@cs.com) if you know of any students in the College Station area who need help.